REVISED

C'EST À TOI!

Level One

Grammar and Vocabulary Exercises

Dianne B. Hopen

Editor
Sarah Vaillancourt

EMC/Paradigm Publishing, Saint Paul, Minnesota

Design and Production: Julie L. Hansen

ISBN 0-8219-1980-6

Published by EMC/Paradigm Publishing
875 Montreal Way
St. Paul, Minnesota 55102
800-328-1452
www.emcp.com
E-mail: educate@emcp.com

Printed in the United States of America
8 9 10 XXX 07 06 05

Contents

Unité 1 *Salut! Ça va?*
Leçon A 1
Leçon B 5

Unité 2 *Qu'est-ce que tu aimes faire?*
Leçon A 9
Leçon B 18
Leçon C 22

Unité 3 *Au café*
Leçon A 27
Leçon B 33
Leçon C 37

Unité 4 *À l'école*
Leçon A 47
Leçon B 53
Leçon C 60

Unité 5 *En famille*
Leçon A 65
Leçon B 71
Leçon C 79

Unité 6 *Tu viens d'où?*
Leçon A 83
Leçon B 91
Leçon C 98

Unité 7 *On fait les magasins.*
Leçon A 105
Leçon B 113
Leçon C 120

Unité 8 *On fait les courses.*
Leçon A 125
Leçon B 132
Leçon C 139

Unité 9 *À la maison*
Leçon A 143
Leçon B 149
Leçon C 158

Unité 10 *La santé*
Leçon A 163
Leçon B 169
Leçon C 177

Unité 11 *En vacances*
Leçon A 183
Leçon B 190
Leçon C 197

Unité 12 *À Paris*
Leçon A 203
Leçon B 211
Leçon C 217

Answers 223

Unité 1 Salut! Ça va?

Leçon A

1 Write seven different French first names. Use each letter in *BONJOUR* as one of the letters in each name.

______________B______________

______________O______________

______________N______________

______________J______________

______________O______________

______________U______________

______________R______________

2 Write five different French last names that you have seen on page 7 in your textbook. Use each letter in *SALUT* as one of the letters in each name.

______________S______________

______________A______________

______________L______________

______________U______________

______________T______________

3 Circle the ten French first names you find in the grid and then write them in the boy's or the girl's column.

P	D	A	V	I	D	A	S	N
G	U	L	N	H	E	L	A	S
A	O	A	D	J	A	D	N	I
Y	M	I	U	A	I	S	A	K
J	H	N	K	A	R	I	N	E
S	A	I	N	O	S	A	D	N
Y	M	E	R	E	J	N	R	S
C	H	J	A	M	D	A	E	I

Boys	Girls
____________	____________
____________	____________
____________	____________
____________	____________
____________	____________

4 Greet each teacher by using the correct French title.

Modèle: Mr. Blanchert
Bonjour, Monsieur.

1. Miss LeClerc ____________________
2. Mrs. Poitras ____________________
3. Mrs. Rémy ____________________
4. Mr. Kourouma ____________________
5. Miss Flambeau ____________________
6. Mr. Diouf ____________________
7. Mrs. Paganelli ____________________
8. Miss François ____________________

5 Greet each student or teacher by using *Bonjour* or *Salut.*

Modèles: *Bonjour*, M. Polizar.
Salut, Bernard.

1. ____________________, Caroline.
2. ____________________, Mlle Ahmel.
3. ____________________, Mme Trudeau.
4. ____________________, Damien.
5. ____________________, M. Colombier.
6. ____________________, Mme Eberhardt.
7. ____________________, Malick.
8. ____________________, Jean-Christophe.

6 Complete each sentence using one of the following words.

je m' TU TE t'

— __________ t'appelles comment?

— __________ m'appelle Max.

— Max, je __________ présente Marie-Alix.

— Pardon, tu __________ appelles comment?

— Je __________ appelle Marie-Alix.

7 Fill in the missing letters to complete the sentences.

— T_____en_____! Je te pr_____s_____nte Khalem.

— _____ar_____on, t_____ t'a_____ _____e_____ _____e_____
c_____mm_____ _____ _____?

— Je _____'app_____ _____ _____e Khalem.

— S_____l_____t, Antoine!

— B_____ _____j_____ur, M_____ _____s_____e_____ _____.

Leçon B

8

Complete each series of numbers by writing the missing ones.

1. deux, quatre, ______ ______ ______
2. cinq, quatre, ______ ______ ______
3. un, trois, ______ ______ ______
4. douze, quatorze, ______ ______ ______
5. onze, treize, ______ ______ ______
6. quatre, huit, ______ ______ ______
7. seize, quinze, ______ ______ ______
8. quatorze, treize, ______ ______ ______

9

Write the number that comes before and after the given number.

1. ______ treize ______
2. ______ huit ______
3. ______ trois ______
4. ______ dix-huit ______
5. ______ douze ______
6. ______ sept ______
7. ______ quatorze ______
8. ______ dix-neuf ______
9. ______ dix-sept ______
10. ______ deux ______

10

Unscramble the following numbers.

1. tpes ____________________
2. zsiee ____________________
3. xdue ____________________
4. gntiv ____________________
5. tzuqeoar ____________________
6. uthi ____________________
7. zqeiun ____________________
8. srito ____________________

11

Find each number spelled out in the grid and circle it.

S	E	I	Z	E	D
E	Z	N	O	I	Q
T	R	E	X	R	G
G	O	U	E	X	T
N	T	F	D	Q	I
I	A	C	I	N	Q
V	U	O	F	R	S
S	Q	S	E	P	T

1. 16
2. 11
3. 7
4. 14
5. 20
6. 5
7. 10
8. 9

12 Complete each addition problem.

Modèle: 4 + 3 = *sept*

1. 2 + 9 = ____________________
2. 3 + 11 = ____________________
3. 7 + 5 = ____________________
4. 6 + 7 = ____________________
5. 8 + 8 = ____________________
6. 1 + 14 = ____________________
7. 17 + 2 = ____________________
8. 4 + 16 = ____________________

13 Complete each subtraction problem.

Modèle: 18 – 5 = *treize*

1. 9 – 4 = ____________________
2. 11 – 8 = ____________________
3. 14 – 7 = ____________________
4. 20 – 3 = ____________________
5. 17 – 13 = ____________________
6. 19 – 1 = ____________________
7. 18 – 9 = ____________________
8. 13 – 7 = ____________________

14

Complete each multiplication problem.

Modèle: 3 x 5 = *quinze*

1. 4 x 2 = ____________________
2. 3 x 4 = ____________________
3. 5 x 2 = ____________________
4. 6 x 3 = ____________________
5. 4 x 5 = ____________________
6. 1 x 2 = ____________________
7. 4 x 4 = ____________________
8. 3 x 3 = ____________________

15

Complete the following conversation in which you, the new exchange student, your teacher and one of your classmates meet and greet each other.

Say hello to Karim, the exchange student. — ____________________, Karim.

Introduce him to M. Roland, your teacher. — Karim, ____________________ M. Roland.

Karim greets the teacher. — ____________________, M. Roland.

M. Roland greets Karim. — ____________________, Karim.

Say hello to Chloé, your classmate. — ____________________, Chloé.

Chloé says hello to the exchange student and asks his name. — ____________________
____

Karim greets Chloé and gives his name. — ____________________
____________________ Karim.

Chloé greets Karim. — ____________________, Karim.

Unité 2 Qu'est-ce que tu aimes faire?

Leçon A

POUR TOI

Subject Pronouns

Do you remember the subject pronouns? They are used to talk to or about people.

Singular		Plural	
je	*I*	**nous**	*we*
tu / **vous**	*you*	**vous**	*you*
il	*he*	**ils** / **elles**	*they*
elle	*she*		
on	*one/they/we*		

1 Valérie gave you a list of the nine subject pronouns in French, but she omitted all the consonants! Add the missing letters to complete each word. Then match it with the letter of its English equivalent.

_______ 1. ____ou____
_______ 2. ____ou____
_______ 3. ____e
_______ 4. i____
_______ 5. o____
_______ 6. e____ ____e
_______ 7. ____u
_______ 8. i____ ____
_______ 9. e____ ____e____

A. they (men and women)
B. they (all women)
C. I
D. we
E. you (one friend)
F. you (more than one friend)
G. he
H. she
I. one/they/we

2 As you read the sentences that follow, you can determine who does which activity by noting the subject pronouns. Write the name(s) of the student(s) being talked about in each sentence.

Denise MYRIAM ET YASMINE

Luc et Sylvie Charles

1. Il aime aller au cinéma. ______
2. Elles regardent la télé. ______
3. Ils écoutent de la musique. ______
4. Elle étudie. ______
5. Ils téléphonent. ______
6. Il joue au basket. ______
7. Elle aime skier. ______
8. Elles nagent. ______

POUR TOI

tu vs. **vous**

When do you use **tu** and when do you use **vous** when talking to one person?

tu	vous
a friend	an adult you don't know
a close relative	a distant relative
a person your age	an older person
a child	an acquaintance
a pet	a person of authority

3 Indicate whether you should use **tu** or **vous** when speaking to the following people.

1. Mlle Blondel ______________________
2. Clément ______________________
3. Louis et Florence ______________________
4. M. Milo ______________________
5. M. et Mme Fertey ______________________
6. Stéphanie ______________________
7. Jeanne et Fabrice ______________________
8. Jean-François ______________________

4 Imagine that you're getting ready for a trip to France. Indicate whether you should use **tu** or **vous** when speaking to the following people.

1. a customs official ______________________
2. your host sister during your French family stay ______________________
3. your French mother upon meeting her ______________________
4. the clerk in a French bakery ______________________
5. your French sister's aunt and uncle ______________________
6. a train conductor ______________________
7. your little French brother ______________________
8. your French sister's English teacher ______________________

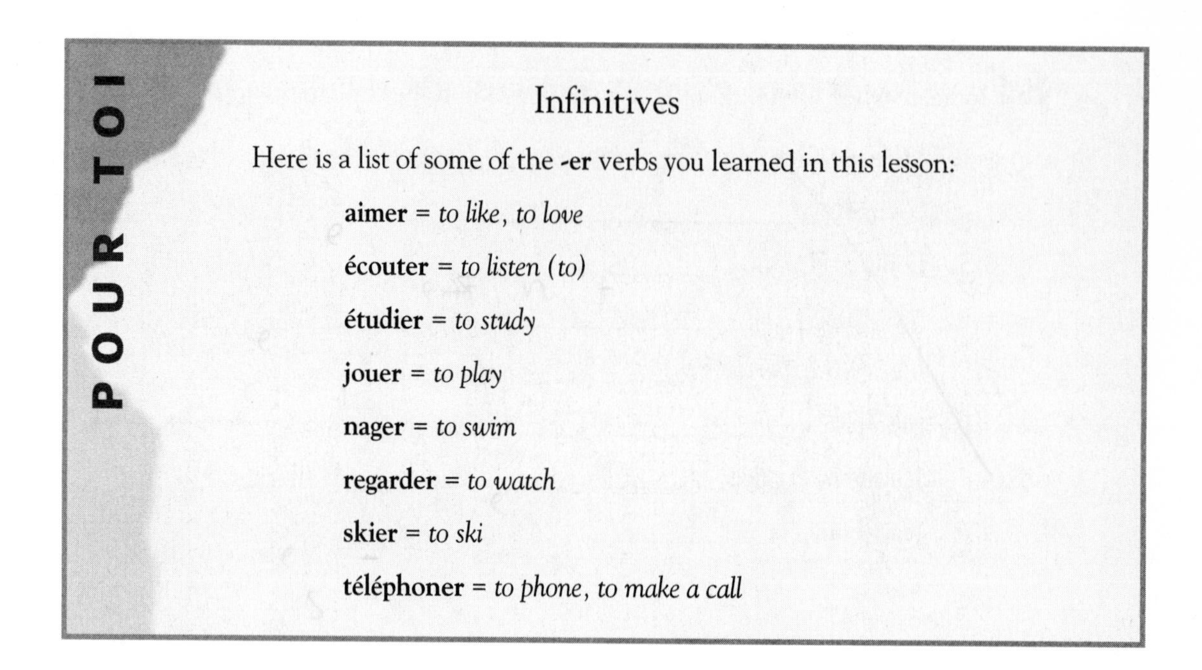

POUR TOI

Infinitives

Here is a list of some of the **-er** verbs you learned in this lesson:

aimer = *to like, to love*

écouter = *to listen (to)*

étudier = *to study*

jouer = *to play*

nager = *to swim*

regarder = *to watch*

skier = *to ski*

téléphoner = *to phone, to make a call*

5 Vincent gave you a list of eight **-er** verbs, but he omitted all the vowels! Add the missing letters to complete each infinitive. Don't forget to add accent marks, when necessary.

1. r_____g_____rd_____r
2. j_____ _____ _____r
3. _____c_____ _____t_____r
4. t_____l_____ph_____n_____r
5. sk_____ _____r
6. _____ _____m_____r
7. n_____g_____r
8. _____t_____d_____ _____r

6 Complete the crossword puzzle with the infinitives you learned in this lesson.

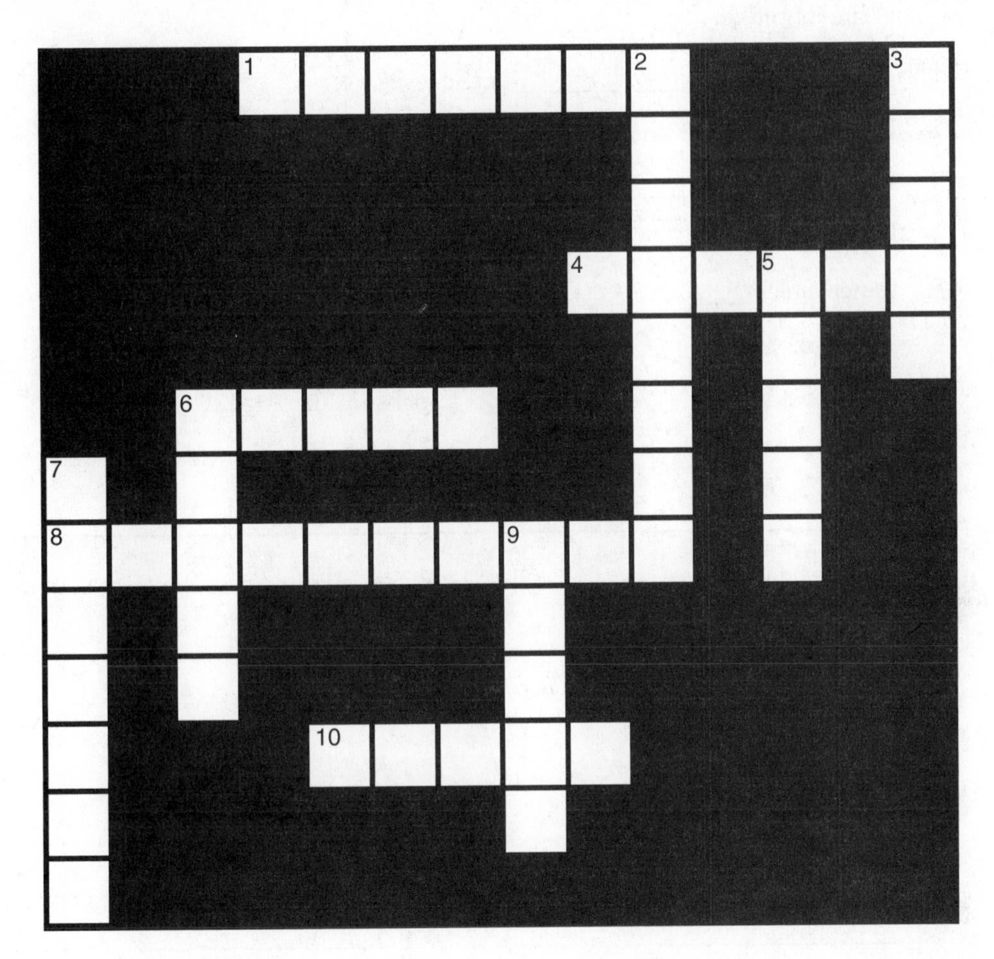

Across

1. to listen (to)
4. to show (a movie)
6. to like, to love
8. to phone, to call
10. to play

Down

2. to watch
3. to do
5. to ski
6. to go
7. to study
9. to swim

7 Tell what Sophie and her friends like to do. Complete each sentence by writing the most appropriate infinitive.

1. J'aime ______________________ la télé.
2. Damien et Martine aiment ______________________ au cinéma.
3. Vous aimez ______________________ de la musique.
4. Françoise aime ______________________ au basket.
5. Renée aime ______________________ au foot.
6. Nous aimons ______________________ pour l'interro.
7. Raphaël aime ______________________ dans (*in*) les Alpes.
8. Francis et Véro aiment ______________________ dans l'océan Atlantique.

8 Rank what you like to do from "1" to "8." ("1" is your favorite.) Use the eight activities mentioned in Activity 7.

Modèles: 1. *J'aime jouer au foot.*
8. *J'aime étudier pour l'interro.*

1. ____
2. ____
3. ____
4. ____
5. ____
6. ____
7. ____
8. ____

9 Using the same set of activities, now tell what your friends and classmates like to do.

Modèles: 1. *Randy aime regarder la télé.*
2. *Heather aime écouter de la musique.*

1. ______________________
2. ______________________
3. ______________________
4. ______________________
5. ______________________
6. ______________________
7. ______________________
8. ______________________

Present tense of regular verbs ending in -er

POUR TOI

To form the present tense of a regular **-er** verb, remove the **-er** and then add the endings that correspond to the subject pronouns.

regarder (*to watch*)

je	regard**e**	nous	regard**ons**
tu	regard**es**	vous	regard**ez**
il/elle/on	regard**e**	ils/elles	regard**ent**

10 Before you do activities in which you write verb forms, complete the following sentences with the appropriate subject pronouns.

1. Pardon, ___tu___ téléphones?
2. Mme Pafundi, ___vous___ aimez écoutez de la musique?
3. Tiens! Cécile et Nadine, ___elles___ jouent au basket.
4. Assia? ___Elle___ nage.
5. ___Nous___ étudions.
6. Merci! ___j___'aime aller au cinéma!
7. Jeanne et Étienne? ___ils___ étudient.
8. Alexandre? ___il___ regarde la télé.

11 In a hurry to finish his homework, Paul left off all the verb endings! Add the missing letter(s) to each verb.

1. Christophe aim<u>e</u> étudier.
2. Damien et Christine jou<u>e</u> <u>n</u> <u>t</u> au basket.
3. Je regard<u>e</u> la télé.
4. Nous aim<u>o</u> <u>n</u> <u>s</u> nager.
5. Mme Duris téléphon<u>e</u>.
6. Sabrina, Anne et Sophie aim<u>e</u> <u>n</u> <u>t</u> aller au cinéma.
7. Vous écout<u>e</u> <u>z</u> de la musique.
8. Tu jou<u>e</u> <u>s</u> au foot.

12 Complete the following sentences with the appropriate form of the indicated verb.

1. (skier) Philippe <u>skie</u> bien.
2. (nager) Vous <u>nagez</u> dans l'océan Pacifique.
3. (jouer) Djamel et Nicolas <u>jouent</u> au basket.
4. (étudier) Nous <u>éstudion.</u> pour l'interro.
5. (aimer) M. et Mme Ferrié <u>aiment</u> aller au cinéma.
6. (jouer) Marie-Claire <u>joue</u> bien au foot.
7. (écouter) Véro et Delphine <u>écoutent</u> de la musique.
8. (regarder) Élisabeth <u>regarde</u> la télé.

13 Complete the crossword puzzle.

Across

4. Elles... au foot?
5. Elle... dans les Alpes.
7. Vous... de la musique?
10. Nous... téléphoner.
12. Jeanne et Michel... de la musique.
14. J'... aller au cinéma.
16. Ils aiment... au cinéma.

Down

1. Il... au basket.
2. M. et Mme Duval... la télé.
3. Vous... nager?
6. Tu... pour l'interro.
7. J'aime... de la musique.
8. Ils aiment aller au....
9. Nous... au basket.
11. Vous... dans les Alpes?
13. Tu... nager?
15. Je... dans l'océan Pacifique.

Leçon B

14 List five activities that teenagers usually do inside and five activities that they usually do outside. Review and use the expressions on pages 20 and 32 of your textbook.

Modèles: Inside: *étudier*
Outside: *faire du vélo*

Inside	Outside
______________________	______________________
______________________	______________________
______________________	______________________
______________________	______________________
______________________	______________________

15 Put a smiley face next to the activities you like to do and a frowning face next to those you don't like to do. Then write a complete sentence for each activity you like to do.

Modèles: 1. aller au cinéma 

2. faire du footing 
J'aime aller au cinéma.

1. écouter le rap
2. étudier
3. faire du vélo
4. jouer au foot
5. faire du sport
6. écouter le jazz
7. faire du roller
8. écouter le rock

____

____

____

____

16 In a note to a classmate, tell what your friends like to do. Write one sentence for each of the following activities.

Modèle: faire du roller
Cindy et Brad aiment faire du roller.

1. faire du sport
2. regarder les films
3. téléphoner
4. écouter le reggae
5. faire du vélo
6. faire du footing
7. écouter de la musique
8. faire du camping

____

____

____

____

____

____

____

____

17 If you were given the choice between two activities, which one would you like to do?

Modèle: écouter de la musique/faire du sport
J'aime faire du sport.

1. faire du roller/faire du camping

____

2. regarder la télé/aller au cinéma

____

3. faire du sport/téléphoner

____

4. jouer au foot/jouer au basket

____

5. écouter la techno/écouter la musique classique

____

6. étudier/faire du vélo

____

7. regarder les films/nager

____

8. skier/faire du footing

____

Position of adverbs

French adverbs usually come right after the verbs they describe.

Sophie aime **bien** faire du roller.

POUR TOI

18 Make your answers in Activity 17 more exact by specifying how much you like each activity. Add **beaucoup**, **bien** or **un peu** to each sentence you wrote.

Modèle: J'aime faire du sport.
J'aime beaucoup faire du sport.

1. ____________________
2. ____________________
3. ____________________
4. ____________________
5. ____________________
6. ____________________
7. ____________________
8. ____________________

19 For each activity you gave as an answer in Activity 17, choose one of your friends or classmates. Tell how much he or she likes that activity.

Modèle: faire du sport
Katie aime un peu faire du sport.

1. ____________________
2. ____________________
3. ____________________
4. ____________________
5. ____________________
6. ____________________
7. ____________________
8. ____________________

Leçon C

20 In the left circle, list activities that you do only after school. In the right circle, list activities that you do only on the weekends. Where the circles intersect, list activities that you do both after school and on the weekends. Review and use the expressions on page 42 of your textbook as well as those on pages 20 and 32.

Modèles: After School: *faire les devoirs*
Weekends: *faire du shopping*
After School and Weekends: *manger*

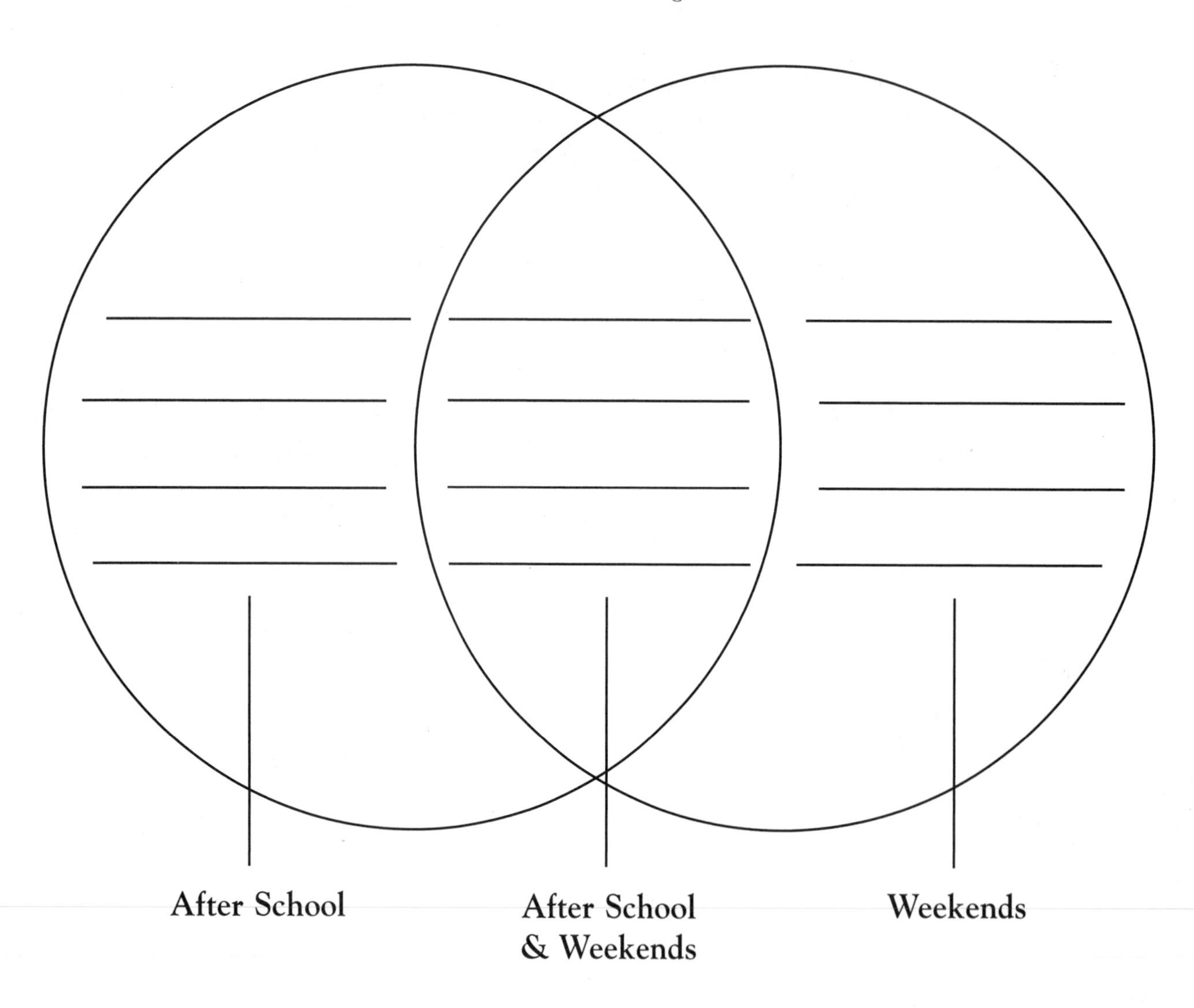

21 Complete the crossword puzzle.

Across

5. Qui n'aime... danser?
6. Qui aime faire les...?
9. Mme Paquette adore... du shopping.
12. J'invite... chez moi.
13. Adam et Alex aiment jouer aux... vidéo.
14. Charles et..., nous aimons skier.

Down

1. M. Thibault n'aime pas...; il aime regarder la télé.
2. On passe un bon film au Gaumont. On y...?
3. J'aime... les films.
4. Nous aimons aller en....
5. Pierre aime le volley, mais il... le foot.
7. Cécile joue... au tennis.
8. Danielle aime... les magazines.
10. J'aime... de la pizza.
11. André Agassi aime jouer au....

POUR TOI

Negation with **ne (n')... pas**

To make a verb negative, put **ne** or **n'** before the verb and **pas** after it.

Patricia **ne** regarde **pas** la télé.

22 None of the following people like the indicated activities. Tell how they feel.

Modèle: Gilberte/lire
Gilberte n'aime pas lire.

1. Sandrine/faire les devoirs

    ____

2. Michel et Louis/faire du shopping

    ____

3. Chloé/jouer au volley

    ____

4. Édouard et Caroline/danser

    ____

5. Céline/sortir

    ____

6. Aïcha/dormir

    ____

7. Abdel-Cader/jouer aux jeux vidéo

    ____

8. Margarette et Latifa/manger de la pizza

    ____

23 The sentences that follow are not true. Rewrite them, changing the negative verbs to the affirmative, and vice versa.

Modèles: Sylvie joue au tennis.
Sylvie ne joue pas au tennis.

Hélène n'aime pas le camping.
Hélène aime le camping.

1. Nous jouons au volley.

 ____

2. Diane ne regarde pas la télé.

 ____

3. Amine n'écoute pas la techno.

 ____

4. Renée et Ariane dansent bien.

 ____

5. Vous ne skiez pas dans les Alpes.

 ____

6. M. et Mme Dumont arrivent le dix.

 ____

7. Tu étudies pour l'interro.

 ____

8. J'aime beaucoup les sports.

 ____

24 Tell whether or not you like to do the following activities.

Modèles: jouer au tennis
J'aime jouer au tennis.

jouer au volley
Je n'aime pas jouer au volley.

1. sortir
____
2. faire les devoirs
____
3. lire
____
4. manger de la pizza
____
5. écouter le jazz
____
6. regarder la télé
____
7. jouer aux jeux vidéo
____
8. faire du shopping
____

Unité 3 Au café

Leçon A

1 How would French speakers respond to the question "Comment vas-tu?" in the following situations? Which expression would each person use?

Très bien. Comme ci, comme ça.
TRÈS MAL. J'AI SOIF. J'ai faim.

1. Philippe is in line at his favorite fast-food restaurant.
____
2. Mme Cousseman has just bought a new outfit.
____
3. Nathalie is studying at the library.
____
4. Khaled is finishing a grueling 20-kilometer run.
____
5. M. Khoretzky is fixing a flat tire on a deserted highway.
____
6. Julien and his friends are at a concert.
____
7. Thierry's mother tells him that dinner won't be ready for two hours.
____
8. Nicolas is walking his dog on a bright, sunny day.
____

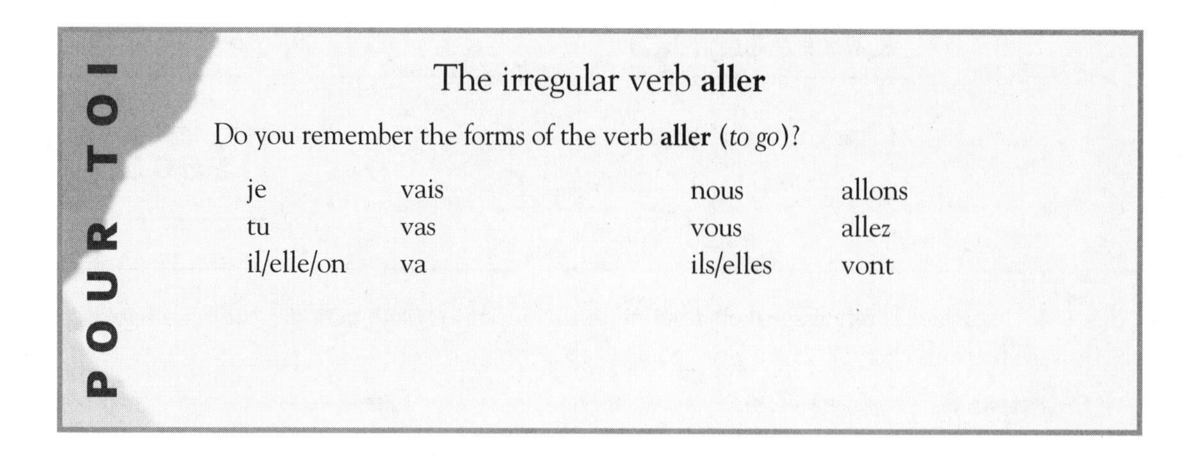

POUR TOI

The irregular verb **aller**

Do you remember the forms of the verb **aller** (*to go*)?

je	vais	nous	allons
tu	vas	vous	allez
il/elle/on	va	ils/elles	vont

2 Complete each form of the subject pronoun and the verb **aller** by adding the missing vowel(s).

1. j____ v____ ____s
2. n____ ____s ____ll____ns
3. ____ls v____nt
4. t____ v____s
5. ____ll____ v____
6. v____ ____s ____ll____z
7. ____l v____
8. ____ll____s v____nt

3 Match each subject with the form of the verb **aller** by writing the letter of the appropriate completion. (Some letters may be used more than once.)

_____ 1. Damien...
_____ 2. Je...
_____ 3. M. et Mme Milo...
_____ 4. Nous...
_____ 5. Tu...
_____ 6. Vous...
_____ 7. Émilie...
_____ 8. Geneviève et Rachel...

A. vais chez moi.
B. allons au café.
C. vas bien?
D. va au fast-food.
E. n'allez pas au cinéma.
F. vont en boîte.

4 Complete each sentence with the appropriate form of the verb **aller**.

Modèle: Sabrina *va* au café.

1. Salima et Théo ____________________ en boîte.
2. Je ____________________ chez moi.
3. Nous n'____________________ pas au cinéma.
4. Raphaël, tu ____________________ au fast-food?
5. Myriam et Alice ____________________ au Macdo.
6. Aïcha et Laurent, vous ____________________ au fast-food ou au café?
7. Monsieur, comment ____________________-vous?

5 Complete the crossword puzzle with either the appropriate subject pronoun or the appropriate form of the verb **aller**.

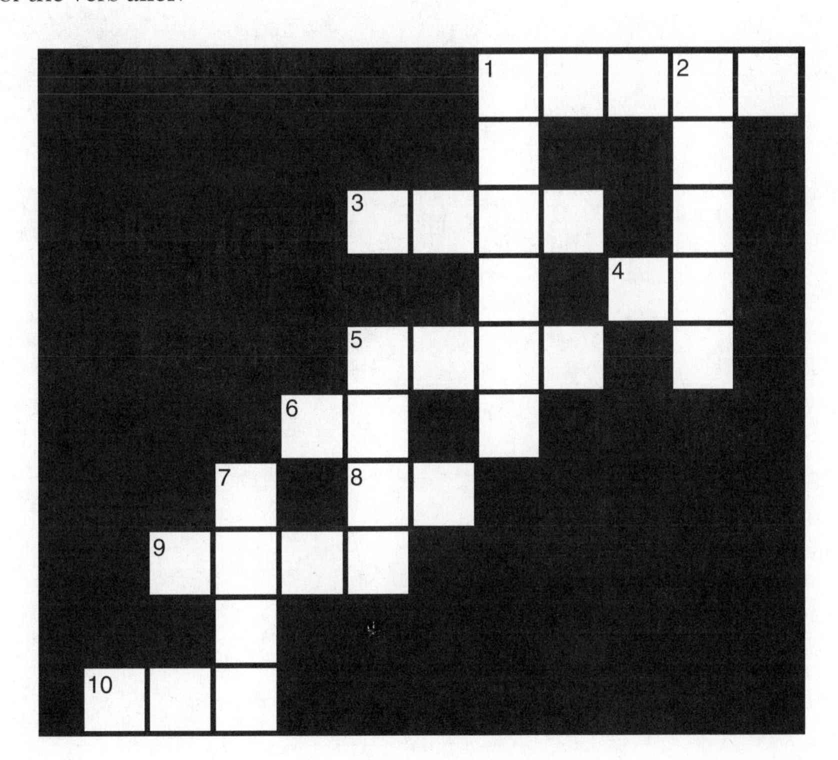

Across

1. Vous... en France.
3. Malika,... va en boîte.
4. ... vais au café.
5. Pierre et Jean-Paul... au Macdo.
6. Ça...?
8. Mahmoud,... va bien.
9. Comment allez-...?
10. Tu... au fast-food.

Down

1. Nous... au restaurant.
2. Sara et Anne,... vont très bien.
5. Je... chez moi.
7. ... n'allons pas au cinéma.

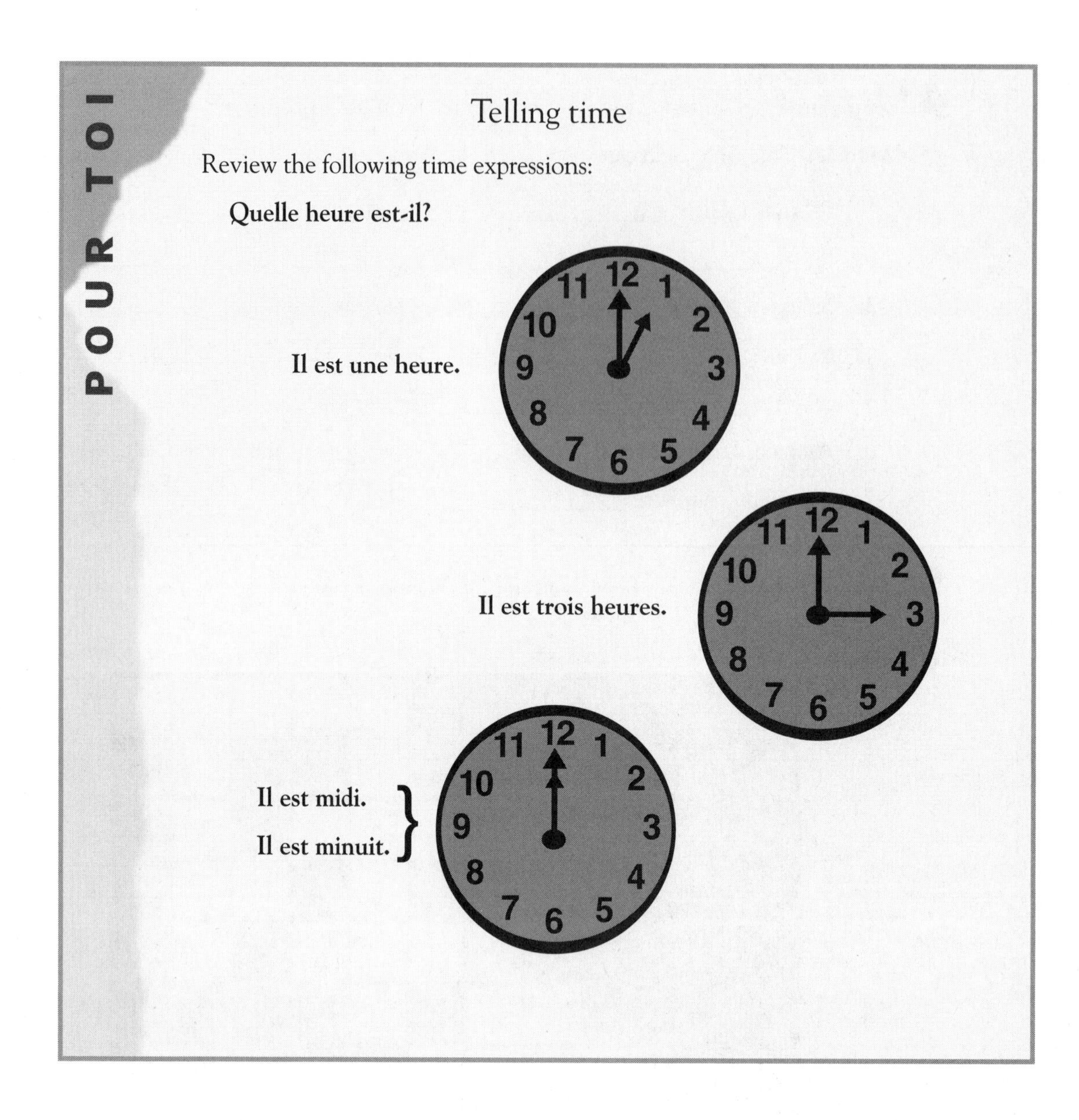

POUR TOI

Telling time

Review the following time expressions:

Quelle heure est-il?

Il est une heure.

Il est trois heures.

Il est midi.
Il est minuit.

6 Label the times in French on the lines beside the numbers. The first one has been done for you.

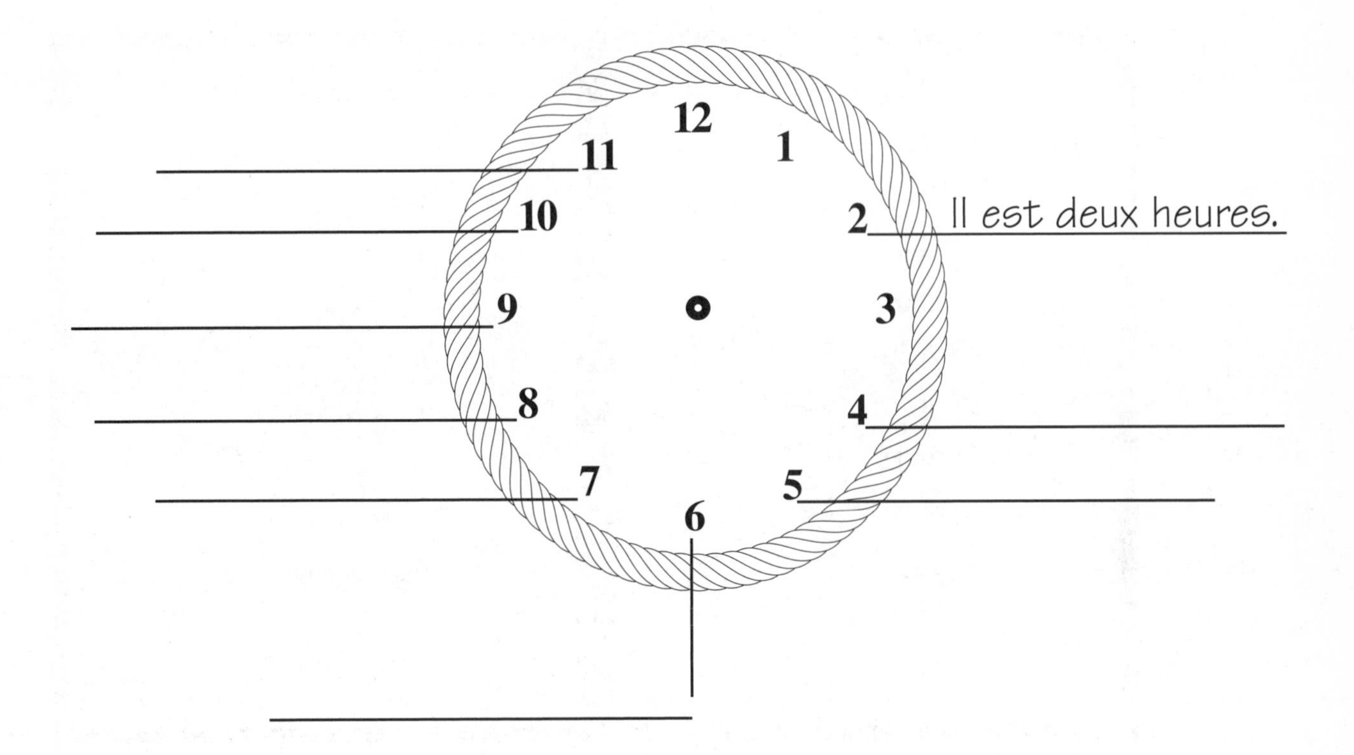

7 Express the following times using numbers.

Modèle: deux heures
2h00

1. six heures ____________
2. une heure ____________
3. neuf heures ____________
4. onze heures ____________
5. sept heures ____________
6. dix heures ____________
7. trois heures ____________
8. cinq heures ____________

8 You have a busy schedule for your first day at a youth retreat. Tell what time it is when you do each of the following activities.

9h00	faire du footing
10h00	lire
11h00	jouer au tennis
12h00	manger
1h00	jouer au basket
2h00	faire du vélo
3h00	jouer au foot
4h00	nager
5h00	jouer au volley
6h00	faire du roller
7h00	danser
8h00	sortir

Modèle: nager
Il est quatre heures.

1. lire ______________________________
2. manger ______________________________
3. faire du vélo ______________________________
4. jouer au foot ______________________________
5. jouer au tennis ______________________________
6. jouer au volley ______________________________
7. faire du footing ______________________________
8. sortir ______________________________

Leçon B

9 Imagine that you're playing Scrabble in French. What food item can you spell with each set of letters?

1. elinalv ____________________
2. mopem ____________________
3. bmnajo ____________________
4. setirf ____________________
5. ssaniir ____________________
6. grenao ____________________
7. merafgo ____________________
8. toohlcca ____________________

10 Categorize the following items by putting each one in the appropriate column.

limonade
hot-dog
glace au chocolat
café
sandwich au fromage
jus de pomme
hamburger
crêpe
jus de raisin
sandwich au jambon
glace à la vanille
jus d'orange
coca
eau minérale

Boissons	Sandwichs	Desserts
____________	____________	____________
____________	____________	____________
____________	____________	____________
____________	____________	____________
____________	____________	____________
____________	____________	____________
____________	____________	____________

11 Find and circle the names of 14 foods and beverages in French.

G	S	V	Y	B	C	U	B	C	R	Y	H	O	Q	I
O	L	E	M	M	O	P	E	D	S	U	J	C	S	V
D	Q	A	T	V	C	D	V	B	W	Q	I	A	N	Q
T	F	U	C	I	A	C	I	X	W	D	N	F	O	E
O	S	M	B	E	R	J	L	B	T	D	X	É	T	R
H	R	I	K	X	A	F	L	Y	W	A	P	T	V	N
V	K	N	T	K	X	U	K	I	H	W	E	Z	X	E
R	X	É	D	J	X	J	C	A	M	L	D	B	G	Q
S	C	R	Ê	P	E	H	M	H	E	L	I	R	X	U
B	A	A	B	F	R	B	G	M	O	T	N	I	Y	I
Y	A	L	K	O	U	M	O	O	R	C	S	A	N	C
M	P	E	A	R	K	V	Y	B	Z	H	O	E	D	H
R	A	M	G	D	G	Y	C	E	A	Q	P	L	B	E
V	L	E	Q	U	E	X	V	I	L	N	B	F	A	R
Y	R	U	W	R	E	U	L	I	L	H	U	Y	O	T

POUR TOI

Gender of nouns and indefinite articles

Nouns in French are either masculine or feminine. **Un** is an indefinite article that precedes a masculine noun; **une** is an indefinite article that precedes a feminine noun.

un steak **une** quiche

12 Categorize the following items by putting each one in the appropriate column. Write **un** or **une** in front of each item.

SANDWICH AU JAMBON coca café quiche
jus d'orange
steak-frites limonade EAU MINÉRALE
crêpe
omelette jus de raisin HOT-DOG salade glace

J'ai faim	J'ai soif

13 Looking at the café menu below, decide what you would order in each situation. Then give your order to the server. Make sure that you don't overspend!

La Carte

une omelette ....5,34 €
une salade ....4,42 €
un steak-frites ......9,91 €
un sandwich au fromage ....4,57 €
un sandwich au jambon ....4,57 €
une quiche ....5,34 €
un hot-dog ....3,81 €
un hamburger..........4,57 €

un café ....3,05 €
un coca ....3,35 €
un jus d'orange ......2,59 €
un jus de pomme ..2,59 €
un jus de raisin ......2,59 €
une limonade ....3,20 €
une eau minérale ..3,35 €

une crêpe ....3,81 €
une glace à la vanille................5,34 €
une glace au chocolat ....5,34 €

Modèle: You invite your best friend out for something to drink. You have 6,86 euros.
Je voudrais un coca et une limonade, s'il vous plaît.

1. You invite a friend to the café for something to eat and drink after class. You have 16,77 euros.

____

2. You stop in the café on a hot day. You have 3,81 euros.

____

3. You invite your French teacher out for dinner. You have 35,06 euros.

____

4. You invite your parents out for dessert. You have 16,77 euros.

____

5. You are in a hurry to get to your afternoon soccer match. You have 7,62 euros.

____

Leçon C

14 Imagine that you're shopping at a Parisian department store. What bills would you give the store clerk if you wanted to buy the following items? (Be sure to give the exact amount.)

Modèle: a pair of shoes for 70 euros
one 50-euro bill and one 20-euro bill

1. a desk for 260 euros

____

2. a TV for 650 euros

____

3. a jacket for 90 euros

____

4. a VCR for 180 euros

____

5. a wallet for 30 euros

____

6. a coat for 135 euros

____

7. four CDs for 85 euros

____

8. a framed painting for 480 euros

____

15 Using the café menu in Activity 13, match each of the orders that follow with the exact amount of money needed to pay for it.

_____ 1. une salade, un hamburger et une limonade

_____ 2. un sandwich au jambon et un sandwich au fromage

_____ 3. une omelette, une crêpe et un café

_____ 4. une quiche et une glace à la vanille

_____ 5. un jus de pomme, un jus de raisin et une limonade

_____ 6. un hot dog, un coca, un jus d'orange et une limonade

_____ 7. un steak-frites et une glace au chocolat

A. un billet de (*of*) dix euros, une pièce de cinquante cents, une pièce de dix cents, une pièce de cinq cents et trois pièces d'un cent

B. un billet de cinq euros, une pièce de deux euros, une pièce d'un euro, une pièce de vingt cents, une pièce de dix cents, une pièce de cinq cents et trois pièces d'un cent

C. un billet de dix euros, un billet de cinq euros, une pièce de vingt cents et une pièce de cinq cents

D. un billet de dix euros, une pièce de deux euros, une pièce de dix cents, une pièce de cinq cents et quatre pièces d'un cent

E. un billet de cinq euros, deux pièces de deux euros, une pièce de dix cents et quatre pièces d'un cent

F. un billet de dix euros, une pièce de deux euros, une pièce de cinquante cents, deux pièces de vingt cents et une pièce de cinq cents

G. un billet de dix euros, une pièce de deux euros et une pièce de vingt cents

POUR TOI

Numbers 20-100

Review the numbers in French from 20 to 100:

20	vingt	30	trente	70	soixante-dix
21	vingt et un	31	trente et un	71	soixante et onze
22	vingt-deux				
23	vingt-trois	40	quarante	80	quatre-vingts
24	vingt-quatre	41	quarante et un	81	quatre-vingt-un
25	vingt-cinq				
26	vingt-six	50	cinquante	90	quatre-vingt-dix
27	vingt-sept	51	cinquante et un	91	quatre-vingt-onze
28	vingt-huit	60	soixante	100	cent
29	vingt-neuf	61	soixante et un		

16 Write out the following numbers in French.

1. 21 ______
2. 72 ______
3. 86 ______
4. 54 ______
5. 100 ______
6. 37 ______
7. 93 ______
8. 65 ______
9. 48 ______

17 Complete each multiplication problem.

Modèle: 5 x 5 = *vingt-cinq*

1. 10 x 8 = ______
2. 6 x 14 = ______
3. 8 x 12 = ______
4. 7 x 9 = ______
5. 12 x 6 = ______
6. 9 x 9 = ______
7. 15 x 6 = ______
8. 6 x 13 = ______

18 Complete the crossword puzzle with the French number that <u>follows</u> the given number.

Across

4. 79
6. 99
7. 49
8. 39
9. 19

Down

1. 89
2. 29
3. 69
5. 59

19 You bought three Loto tickets.

Here is a list of this week's winning Loto numbers. Circle any of the winning numbers that appear on your three cards. Do you have a winning card? Which one?

quarante-six	vingt-quatre	trente-trois
soixante-seize	quarante-sept	soixante-cinq
cinquante-cinq	cinquante-six	soixante et onze
vingt-neuf	soixante-douze	trente-neuf
quatre-vingt-huit	quatre-vingt-un	soixante-dix-huit

20 Write out the number that comes before and after the given number.

1. ____________ cinquante-huit ____________
2. ____________ trente-deux ____________
3. ____________ soixante-quinze ____________
4. ____________ quatre-vingt-dix-neuf ____________
5. ____________ soixante-deux ____________
6. ____________ quatre-vingt-deux ____________
7. ____________ vingt-six ____________
8. ____________ quatre-vingt-dix ____________

21 Your class is going to play bingo. To help you during the game, write out the numbers on your bingo card.

B	I	N	G	O
12 ____	22 ____	41 ____	47 ____	71 ____
4 ____	19 ____	39 ____	46 ____	75 ____
8 ____	16 ____	34 ____	58 ____	62 ____
13 ____	26 ____	32 ____	43 ____	70 ____
11 ____	28 ____	45 ____	51 ____	66 ____

22 Complete the crossword puzzle with the answers to the math problems.

Across

1. 72 – 47 =
3. 63 ÷ 9 =
4. 36 + 27 =
6. 24 + 16 =
7. 13 x 6 =
8. 100 – 19 =
10. 7 x 7 =
11. 48 ÷ 4 =

Down

2. 97 – 42 =
3. 80 ÷ 5 =
5. 58 – 24 =
9. 25 x 4 =

POUR TOI

Definite articles

The singular definite articles are **le**, **la** and **l'**. **Le** precedes a masculine word; **la** precedes a feminine word; **l'** precedes a word that begins with a vowel sound.

le chocolat **la** limonade **l'**eau minérale

Il replaces a masculine singular noun; **elle** replaces a feminine singular noun.

23 Complete the first sentence in each pair with **Le**, **La** or **L'**. Complete the second one with **Il** or **Elle**.

Modèle: *Le* hot-dog est bon. *Il* coûte 3,96 €.

1. ________ jus d'orange est pour Cécile. ________ coûte 2,74 €.
2. ________ pizza est super. ________ coûte 3,81 €.
3. ________ omelette est délicieuse. ________ coûte 5,34 €.
4. ________ steak-frites est superbe. ________ coûte 10,67 €.
5. ________ glace à la vanille est bonne. ________ coûte 5,03 €.
6. ________ coca est frais. ________ coûte 2,74 €.
7. ________ sandwich au fromage est bon. ________ coûte 4,27 €.
8. ________ eau minérale est fraîche. ________ coûte 3,05 €.

24 Imagine that you're a server in a small French restaurant. A client asks you to tell him what's on the menu and how much each item costs, since the only menu is posted too far away for him to read.

La Carte

Steak-frites	10,21€
Sandwich au jambon	4,42€
Sandwich au fromage	4,27€
Crêpe	4,57€
Glace à la vanille	4,88€
Glace au chocolat	5,18€
Coca	3,35€
Thé	3,05€
Limonade	3,20€

Modèle: coca
Le coca coûte trois euros trente-cinq.

1. sandwich au jambon

____

2. thé

____

3. glace au chocolat

____

4. crêpe

____

5. sandwich au fromage

____

6. limonade

____

7. steak-frites

____

8. glace à la vanille

____

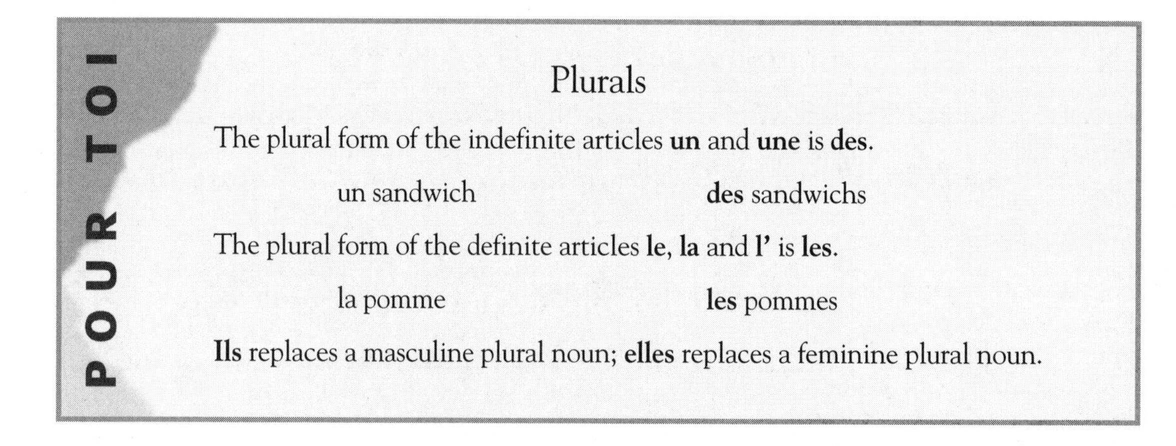

POUR TOI

Plurals

The plural form of the indefinite articles **un** and **une** is **des**.

un sandwich → **des** sandwichs

The plural form of the definite articles **le**, **la** and **l'** is **les**.

la pomme → **les** pommes

Ils replaces a masculine plural noun; **elles** replaces a feminine plural noun.

25 Complete the following conversations using **ils**, **elles**, **les** or **des**.

1. — Combien coûtent _______________ sandwichs au fromage?
   — _______________ coûtent 8,30 €.
2. — Vous désirez _______________ raisins?
   — Oui, mais _______________ coûtent combien?
3. — J'aime _______________ desserts. Et toi?
   — Oui, je voudrais _______________ crêpes. _______________ coûtent 6,60 €.
4. — Je voudrais _______________ boissons.
   — Voyons... _______________ coûtent 10,25 €.
5. — J'aime _______________ quiches.
   — Moi, aussi. _______________ sont délicieuses.

Unité 4 À l'école

Leçon A

1 Make a list of the objects pictured on pages 96 and 97 of your textbook that could be found in the places that follow. Put each object in only one category.

sur un bureau	sur une table d'étudiant	dans un sac à dos

2 List as many school items as you can in French that you have with you today.

Modèle: *J'ai trois livres et un crayon.*

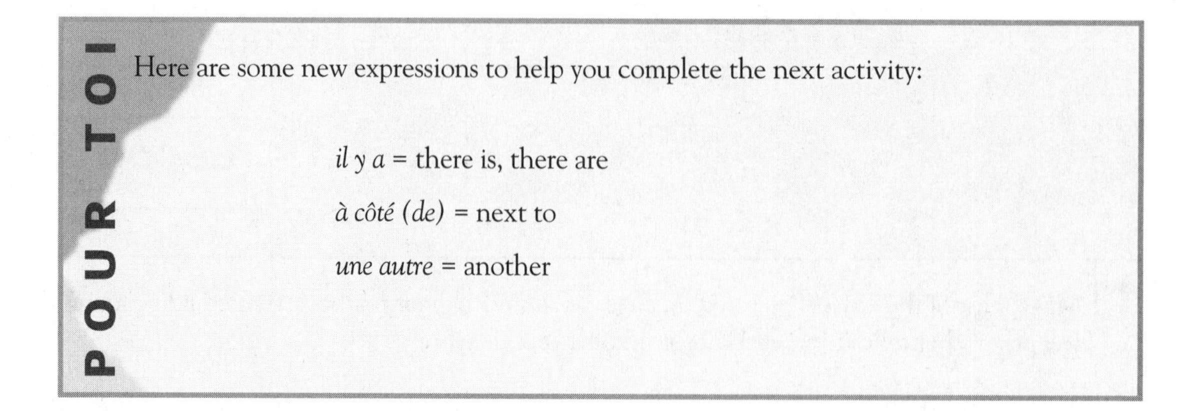

Here are some new expressions to help you complete the next activity:

il y a = there is, there are

à côté (de) = next to

une autre = another

3 Read the classroom description that follows, then draw this scene. Finally, write the French name of each object you have drawn next to it.

C'est une salle de classe avec deux fenêtres. Il y a quatre tables et quatre chaises pour les étudiants. Devant la salle de classe il y a un bureau pour le professeur, et derrière le bureau il y a un tableau et deux affiches. Sur le bureau il y a un ordinateur et deux disquettes. Sur une table d'étudiant il y a un sac à dos. Devant le sac à dos il y a trois cahiers et un livre. Sur le sac à dos il y a un dictionnaire. Sur une autre table d'étudiant il y a une trousse et avec la trousse il y a trois crayons.

Present tense of the irregular verb **avoir**

Do you remember the forms of the verb **avoir** (*to have*)?

j'	ai	nous	avons
tu	as	vous	avez
il/elle/on	a	ils/elles	ont

POUR TOI

4 Tell what classroom objects everyone has by writing the letter of the appropriate verb form to complete each sentence. (Some letters may be used more than once.)

_____ 1. Sandrine et Manu ____ deux cahiers.

_____ 2. J'____ une trousse et des crayons.

_____ 3. Nous ____ les disquettes pour l'ordinateur.

_____ 4. L'élève ____ des affiches.

_____ 5. Vous ____ un sac à dos.

_____ 6. Tu ____ les cassettes.

_____ 7. Les professeurs ____ des magnétoscopes dans les salles de classe.

_____ 8. Louis ____ un livre de maths.

A. ai
B. avez
C. a
D. ont
E. avons
F. as

5 Complete the crossword puzzle with either the appropriate subject pronoun or the appropriate form of the verb **avoir**.

Across

1. M. Leclerc... un ordinateur.
3. ... avez une question?
4. J'... besoin d'étudier.
6. ... avons un bon professeur.
7. Anne et Laure,... n'ont pas les devoirs.

Down

1. Nous... besoin de sortir.
2. ... as une trousse?
4. Vous n'... pas le stylo?
5. Bernard,... a dix francs?

6 Answer each question with a complete sentence.

Modèle: Tu as des livres dans ce (*this*) sac à dos?
Oui, j'ai des livres dans ce sac à dos.

1. Le professeur a un ordinateur dans la salle de classe?

____

2. Les élèves ont des livres dans leurs (*their*) sacs à dos?

____

3. Tu as des crayons ou des stylos?

____

4. La salle de classe a quinze fenêtres?

____

5. Le professeur a des vidéocassettes pour le magnétoscope?

____

6. Vous avez une pendule dans la salle de classe?

____

7. Les élèves ont les devoirs dans leurs cahiers?

____

8. Tu as un sac à dos?

____

7 Complete each sentence with the most appropriate expression.

besoin	soif	FAIM

1. Marie-Alix a _______________. Elle mange un sandwich.
2. J'ai _______________ d'un stylo pour l'interro.
3. Vous avez _______________! Vous avez dix crêpes.
4. M. Ferrié a _______________ d'une disquette pour l'ordinateur.
5. Les élèves ont _______________. Ils ont de l'eau minérale.
6. Jean et Karina ont _______________ d'étudier. Ils ont une interro.
7. Nous avons _______________. Nous avons des boissons.
8. Tu as _______________. Tu vas au fast-food.

8 Compose a logical sentence with each set of words.

Modèle: faim/avons/oui/nous
Oui, nous avons faim.

1. besoin/vous/d'/avez/livre/un

 ____

2 avec/dos/dictionnaire/à/le/sac/est/le

 ____

3. tableau/derrière/la/est/prof/le

 ____

4. dans/vidéocassette/magnétoscope/le/la/est

 ____

5. bureau/sur/ordinateur/le/est/l'

 ____

6. soif/et/Bernier/M./ont/Mme

 ____

7. classe/taille-crayon/le/de/salle/la/dans/est

 ____

8. ai/papier/une/de/j'/feuille

 ____

Leçon B

9 Imagine that you're playing Scrabble in French. Which day of the week can you spell with each set of letters?

1. imsdea ____________________
2. drcmiree ____________________
3. iduej ____________________
4. hicmeadn ____________________
5. irmda ____________________
6. ddeevinr ____________________
7. inuld ____________________

10 Match each day of the week in English with its counterpart in French by writing the appropriate letter.

_____ 1. Monday
_____ 2. Tuesday
_____ 3. Wednesday
_____ 4. Thursday
_____ 5. Friday
_____ 6. Saturday
_____ 7. Sunday

A. samedi
B. mercredi
C. vendredi
D. lundi
E. dimanche
F. jeudi
G. mardi

11 Complete the crossword puzzle with the names of various courses that schools offer. Each clue gives the first two letters of the course; you must write the full name of the course. You may first want to review the vocabulary on page 106 of your textbook.

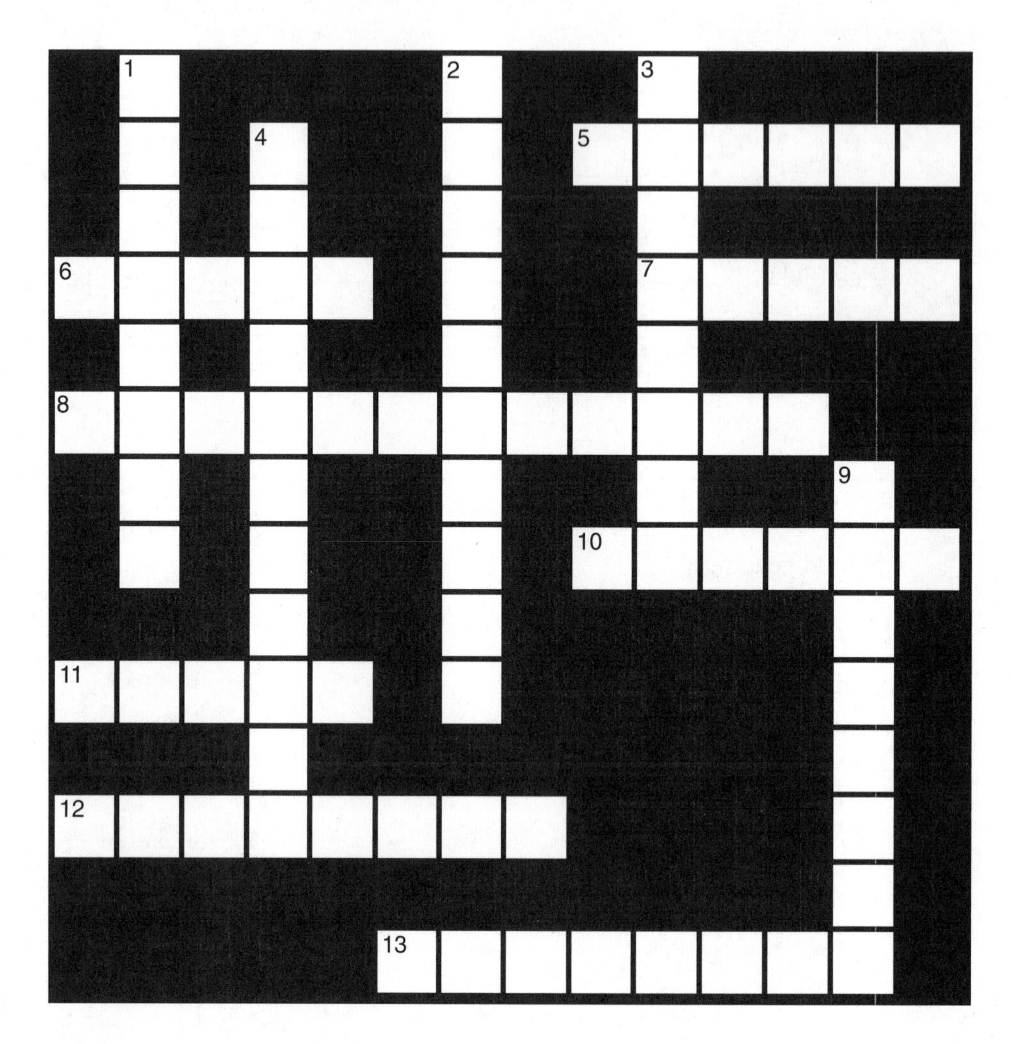

Across

5. la ch...
6. le la...
7. le sp...
8. l'in...
10. le de...
11. les ma...
12. l'al...
13. la bi...

Down

1. l'es...
2. la gé...
3. la ph...
4. la ph...
9. l'hi...

12 Put each of the following school courses in the appropriate category.

l'histoire	la chimie	le dessin	le français
la géographie	le latin	l'anglais	la philosophie
la physique	l'allemand	l'espagnol	la musique
la biologie			

les arts	les langues (*languages*)	les sciences	les sciences sociales (*social sciences*)

POUR TOI

Present tense of regular verbs ending in -ir

To form the present tense of a regular **-ir** verb, remove the **-ir** and then add the endings that correspond to the subject pronouns.

finir (*to finish*)

je	fini**s**	nous	fin**issons**
tu	fini**s**	vous	fin**issez**
il/elle/on	fini**t**	ils/elles	fin**issent**

13

Complete each form of the subject pronoun and the verb **finir** by adding the missing vowel(s).

1. t____ f____n____s
2. ____ls f____n____ss____nt
3. j____ f____n____s
4. n____ ____s f____n____ss____ns
5. ____ll____s f____n____ss____nt
6. ____n f____n____t
7. v____ ____s f____n____ss____z
8. ____ll____ f____n____t

14

Céline and her friends all have tests today. Using the appropriate form of **finir**, say what test everyone is finishing at the end of the first hour.

Modèle: Valérie *finit* l'interro de maths.

1. Céline ______________________________ l'interro de philosophie.
2. Sandrine et Élisabeth ______________________________ l'interro d'histoire.
3. Vous ______________________________ l'interro d'anglais.
4. Je ______________________________ l'interro de français.
5. Nathalie et Hervé ______________________________ l'interro d'informatique.
6. Tu ______________________________ l'interro de musique.
7. Damien ______________________________ l'interro de biologie.
8. Nous ______________________________ l'interro de français.

Other -ir verbs

POUR TOI

Here are some other regular **-ir** verbs that follow the same pattern as **finir**.

choisir = *to choose*

grossir = *to get fat, to gain weight*

maigrir = *to get thin, to lose weight*

obéir = *to obey*

punir = *to punish*

remplir = *to fill (out)*

réussir = *to succeed, to pass (a test)*

15 Complete the crossword puzzle with regular **-ir** verbs.

Across

3. to fill
5. to obey
6. to choose
7. to punish

Down

1. to gain weight
2. to lose weight
4. to succeed

16 Everyone is talking about the new classes they have selected for next year. Complete each sentence with the appropriate form of the verb **choisir**.

Modèle: Fatima *choisit* la biologie.

1. Nous ____________________ le français, les maths et l'histoire.
2. Zohra et Yasmine ____________________ le sport et le dessin.
3. Je ____________________ l'informatique et la chimie.
4. Vous ____________________ l'histoire, la biologie et le latin.
5. Isabelle, Éric et Normand ____________________ la philosophie et l'histoire.
6. Clémence ____________________ l'allemand et l'informatique.
7. Fayçal ____________________ l'anglais et l'espagnol.
8. Tu ____________________ la musique et le dessin.

17 At the annual school fair the French students have set up the booth "Show What You Know." You must pick a subject pronoun card and then match it with the appropriate sentence. For each sentence, list all the possible subject pronouns.

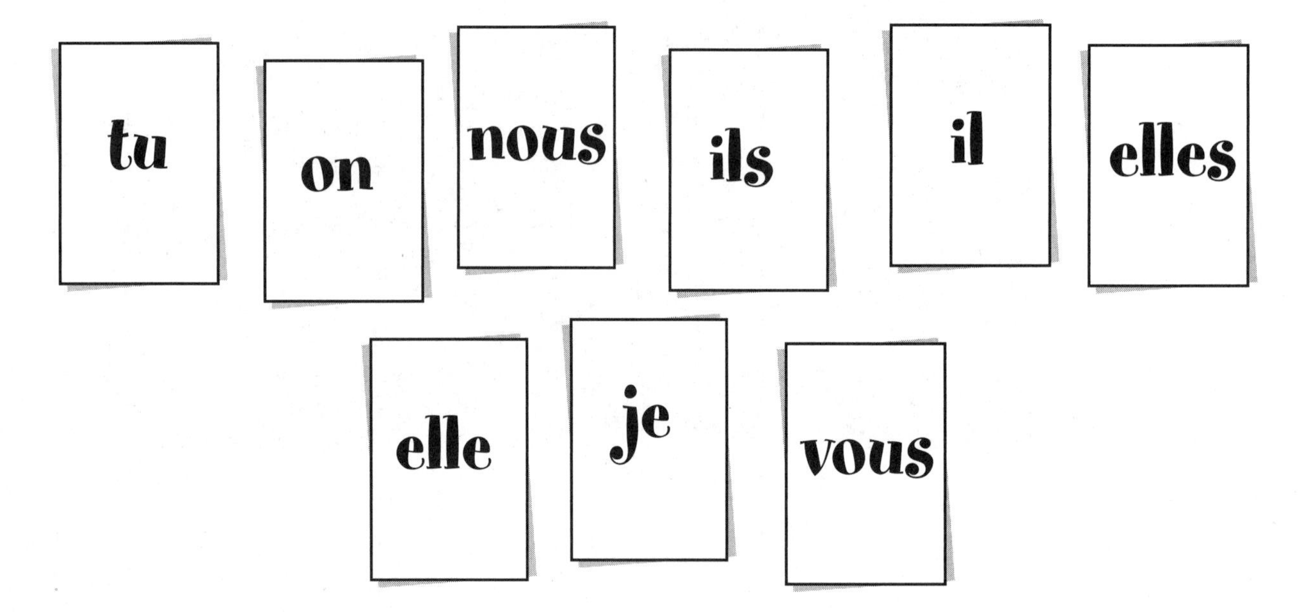

1. _____ ne réussissons pas à l'interro d'allemand.
2. Amine est un bon élève. _____ obéit au professeur.
3. Après (*after*) dix pizzas, _____ grossis!

4. Et _____ choisissez les crêpes?
5. Jasmine et Magali, _____ réussissent toujours (*always*).
6. _____ punit les élèves.
7. _____ maigrissez!
8. _____ remplis l'eau minérale.

18

Complete the following sentences with the appropriate form of the indicated verb.

1. (punir) Le professeur ne ______________________________ pas les étudiants.
2. (obéir) Nous ______________________________ toujours.
3. (maigrir) Sonia et Assia ______________________________!
4. (remplir) Tu ______________________________le coca.
5. (grossir) Édouard et Catherine mangent beaucoup! Ils ________________________!
6. (réussir) Pierre ne ______________________________ pas à l'interro.
7. (finir) Je ______________________________ les devoirs après les cours.
8. (choisir) Vous ______________________________ le français et le latin.

19

Before you practice telling time in *Leçon C*, review the numbers from 1 to 60. Then write out the following numbers.

1. 5 ____
2. 20 ____
3. 15 ____
4. 10 ____
5. 25 ____
6. 40 ____
7. 53 ____
8. 58 ____

Leçon C

POUR TOI

Telling exact time

Do you remember how to tell exact time in French?

1h00	Il est une heure.
1h05	Il est une heure cinq.
1h15	Il est une heure et quart. Il est une heure quinze.
1h20	Il est une heure vingt.
1h30	Il est une heure et demie. Il est une heure trente.
1h35	Il est une heure trente-cinq. Il est deux heures moins vingt-cinq.
1h45	Il est une heure quarante-cinq. Il est deux heures moins le quart.
1h55	Il est une heure cinquante-cinq. Il est deux heures moins cinq.

20 Write out the time using the 24-hour system.

Modèle: 2h00 ☼
Il est quatorze heures.

1. 4h00 ☼ ______________________
2. 8h00 ☾ ______________________
3. 1h00 ☼ ______________________
4. 3h00 ☼ ______________________
5. 9h00 ☾ ______________________
6. 11h00 ☼ ______________________
7. 1h00 ☾ ______________________
8. 12h00 ☼ ______________________

21 Match the time on the clock with the letter of its written description.

_____ 1.

_____ 2. 12:35

_____ 3.

_____ 4.

_____ 5.

_____ 6. 1:25

_____ 7.

_____ 8.

A. Il est onze heures cinq.

B. Il est deux heures moins vingt.

C. Il est une heure vingt-cinq.

D. Il est trois heures moins le quart.

E. Il est quatre heures dix.

F. Il est cinq heures moins dix.

G. Il est une heure moins vingt-cinq.

H. Il est trois heures et quart.

22 With each set of words, compose a logical sentence about what time it is.

1. heure/quart/est/moins/il/une/le

 ____

2. midi/demi/est/et/il

 ____

3. il/quart/et/est/heures/cinq

 ____

4. est/cinq/cinq/heures/il

 ____

5. neuf/trente/heures/est/il

 ____

6. moins/il/minuit/est/vingt

 ____

7. vingt-cinq/heures/il/six/est

 ____

8. heures/sept/il/quart/et/est

 ____

23 Thérèse's watch needs a new battery, so she seldom knows the correct time. When she asks you if her watch is right, check the digital clock and then answer her.

Modèles: Il est neuf heures cinq?
Oui, il est neuf heures cinq.

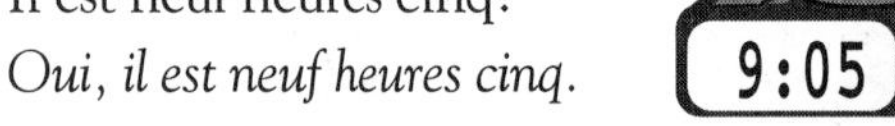

Il est onze heures dix?
Non, il est onze heures vingt.

1. Il est huit heures cinq?

 ____

2. Il est neuf heures et quart?

 ____

3. Il est sept heures et quart?

____

4. Il est trois heures et demie?

____

5. Il est sept heures moins le quart?

____

6. Il est onze heures dix?

____

7. Il est cinq heures et quart?

____

8. Il est quatre heures moins cinq?

____

24 Write out your daily class schedule.

Modèle: *À huit heures et quart, j'ai français.*

____

____

____

____

____

____

____

____

25 Answer the following questions.

Modèle: Tu as français à quelle heure?
J'ai français à huit heures et quart.

1. Tu arrives à l'école à quelle heure?

____

2. Tu as anglais à quelle heure?

____

3. Tu vas à la cantine à quelle heure?

____

4. Tu étudies à quelle heure?

____

5. Tu regardes la télé à quelle heure?

____

6. Tu écoutes la radio à quelle heure?

____

7. Tu manges avec la famille à quelle heure?

____

8. Tu vas au cinéma à quelle heure?

____

Unité 5 En famille

Leçon A

1 Match each masculine family member with the letter of the feminine equivalent. You may first want to review the vocabulary on pages 133 and 135 of your textbook.

_____ 1. le père
_____ 2. le frère
_____ 3. le cousin
_____ 4. l'oncle
_____ 5. le demi-frère
_____ 6. le fils
_____ 7. le beau-père
_____ 8. le beau-frère

A. la mère
B. la demi-sœur
C. la cousine
D. la belle-mère
E. la sœur
F. la tante
G. la belle-sœur
H. la fille

2 Read the description of Laurent's family. Then complete the sentences, using each of the listed words only once.

ANS ai roux BLONDS
yeux ONT cheveux
a âge noirs

J'_____________________ seize ans. J'ai les cheveux _____________________ et les _____________________ bleus. Mes (*my*) deux sœurs _____________________ treize ans et neuf ans, et elles ont les _____________________ bruns. Mon père, qui a quarante-deux _____________________, a les cheveux _____________________. Ma mère, qui _____________________ quarante et un ans, a les cheveux _____________________.

Et toi? Tu as quel _____________________?

3 In the grid, circle the 22 French expressions for names of family members that you find on page 133 of your textbook. Then write each one (with **un** or **une**) in the appropriate column.

```
M E R È R F U A E B A L W I D
T E R È R F I M E D T E R D O
E L C N O G I L R V R A N G V
R D Y O K B L W È È M Y N W F
È G E G U E E L P A R E N T S
M Q R R S S B Y D S F I L L E
F G U O È E I E N I S U O C Y
R Y E R È M D N A R G O T F A
È U O I S O E U R U B L E A F
R Y S L B D D L G Z P M Z L J
E D I M J I G P L R M È W L R
S F M S T N A F N E W D R O S
A J E A X P F K K M B B M E P
J I D J W Y Z T V E G L M V N
```

Male	Female
______________________	______________________
______________________	______________________
______________________	______________________
______________________	______________________
______________________	______________________
______________________	______________________
______________________	______________________
______________________	______________________

4 Write a short paragraph about yourself and three of your family members. Give everyone's name and age. Also tell the color of their hair and eyes.

Modèle: *Ma belle-mère s'appelle Cathy. Elle a trente-huit ans. Elle a les cheveux....*

POUR TOI

Possessive adjectives

	Masculine	Feminine (before consonant)	Feminine (before vowel)	Plural
my	**mon**	**ma**	**mon**	**mes**
your	**ton**	**ta**	**ton**	**tes**
his, her, one's, its	**son**	**sa**	**son**	**ses**
our	**notre**	**notre**	**notre**	**nos**
your	**votre**	**votre**	**votre**	**vos**
their	**leur**	**leur**	**leur**	**leurs**

Remember that a possessive adjective agrees with the noun that follows it.

C'est **mon** frère. C'est **ma** sœur.

5 You and many of your friends and family members are at a local café. Tell what everyone has on the table in front of them by writing the letter of the appropriate completion. (Some sentences may have two possible completions.)

___ 1. Mon père a...
___ 2. Tu as...
___ 3. Ma sœur a...
___ 4. J'ai...
___ 5. Vous avez...
___ 6. Ma tante et ma belle-mère ont...
___ 7. Nous avons...
___ 8. Jean-Philippe et Suzanne ont...

A. leurs sandwichs.
B. ma pizza.
C. votre hamburger.
D. ses frites.
E. nos boissons.
F. sa glace à la vanille.
G. ta limonade.
H. leurs desserts.

6 Everyone at a national French contest test on Saturday morning comes with their own supplies to help them prepare for or take the test. Tell what everyone has with them by completing the following sentences with the appropriate possessive adjectives.

1. J'ai mon cahiers et mon sac à dos.
2. Abdou a ton crayons et ta livre de français.
3. Marie-Claire et Adja ont leurs trousses et leurs stylos.
4. Nous avons nos cassettes et notre dictionnaire.
5. Tu as tes livres et ton crayon.
6. Claudette a son stylo et sa cassette.
7. Vous avez votre livre et vos cahiers.
8. Le professeur a sa magnétoscope et sa vidéocassette.

POUR TOI

Expressions with **avoir**

Review the following expressions used to ask and tell someone's age.

Tu as quel âge?	Ton frère a quel âge?
J'ai treize ans.	Il a quinze ans.

7 Ask your classmate Ariane about the ages of some of her family members. Complete each sentence with the appropriate word.

1. — Ton père a ________ âge?
   — Il a quarante-cinq ________.
2. — Ta mère ________ quel âge?
   — ________ a quarante et un ans.
3. — Ta sœur a quel ________?
   — Elle ________ douze ans.
4. — Ton beau-frère a ________ âge?
   — Il a dix-huit ________.

5. — Tes cousines ______________________ quel âge?

— ______________________ ont seize ans.

6. — Tu ______________________ quel âge?

— J'______________________ ______________________ ans.

8 Éric, the French exchange student, is telling you about his family. Unfortunately, you don't hear everyone's ages. Ask Éric to repeat what he has said.

Modèle: Ma tante a trente-sept ans.
Ta tante a quel âge?

1. Mon oncle a trente-neuf ans.

   ____

2. Ma belle-sœur a dix-neuf ans.

   ____

3. Mon beau-frère a dix ans.

   ____

4. Mes parents ont quarante-six ans.

   ____

5. Ma grand-mère a soixante-huit ans.

   ____

6. Mon grand-père a soixante-dix ans.

   ____

7. Mon cousin a seize ans.

   ____

8. Ma cousine a dix-huit ans.

   ____

Leçon B

9 Imagine that you're playing Scrabble in French. Which month of the year can you spell with each set of letters?

1. ervéfir
2. ijnu
3. mrcdbeeé
4. rcoobte
5. samr
6. ltieluj
7. lairv
8. mbeonevr
9. taûo
10. vneairj
11. ami
12. metsrebpe

10

Match each month of the year in English with its counterpart in French by writing the appropriate letter.

_____	1. January	A.	mars
_____	2. February	B.	juin
_____	3. March	C.	août
_____	4. April	D.	novembre
_____	5. May	E.	mai
_____	6. June	F.	janvier
_____	7. July	G.	décembre
_____	8. August	H.	juillet
_____	9. Septembre	I.	avril
_____	10. October	J.	septembre
_____	11. November	K.	février
_____	12. December	L.	octobre

11

Looking through a French home furnishings catalogue, you see various pieces of furniture and their prices in euros. Write out the price of each item or set of items.

Modèle: two velvet love seats
mille sept cent trente-cinq euros

1. computer armoire and two bookshelves

____

2. dining table, hutch and six chairs

____

3. two bedroom sets

____

4. patio furniture

____

5. entertainment center

____

6. large-screen TV

____

7. four marble end tables and matching marble coffee table

____

8. two leather sofas

____

12

Match the price of each house with the letter of its price written in words.

_____ 1.

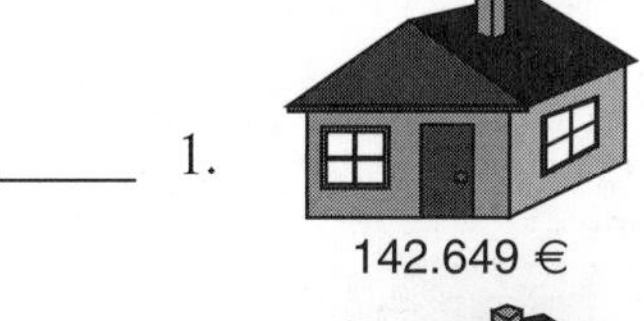

_____ 2.

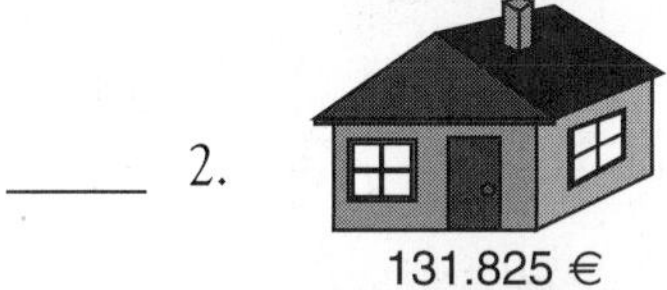

_____ 3.

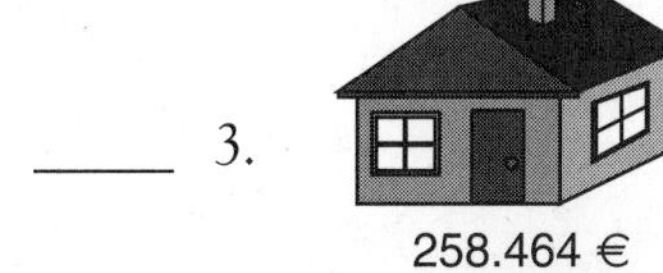

_____ 4.

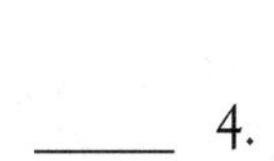

_____ 5.

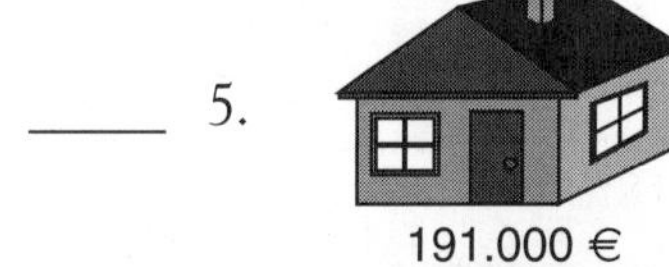

_____ 6.

_____ 7.

_____ 8.

A. deux cent cinquante-huit mille quatre cent soixante-quatre euros

B. cent quatre-vingt-onze mille euros

C. un million cent dix mille cinq cent cinquante-cinq euros

D. cent quarante-deux mille six cent quarante-neuf euros

E. cent soixante six mille six cent quarante-sept euros

F. deux cent vingt-neuf mille trois cent huit euros

G. cent trente et un mille huit cent vingt-cinq euros

H. cent cinq mille neuf cent quarante-deux euros

---

13 Tell what pet(s) each person has.

Modèle:

Sophie a deux chats.

1. 

____

2. 

____

3. 

____

4. 

____

5. 

____

6. 

____

7. 

____

8. 

____

POUR TOI

Present tense of the irregular verb **être**

Do you remember the forms of the verb **être** (*to be*)?

je	suis	nous	sommes
tu	es	vous	êtes
il/elle/on	est	ils/elles	sont

14 Match each subject with the form of the verb **être** by writing the letter of the appropriate completion.

_____ 1. C'...

_____ 2. Nous...

_____ 3. Charlotte et Jean-Paul...

_____ 4. Tu...

_____ 5. La Martinique et la Guadeloupe...

_____ 6. La prof...

_____ 7. Je...

_____ 8. Vous...

A. sommes lundi.

B. sont en vacances.

C. est le 11 octobre.

D. suis très intelligent!

E. êtes de Pointe-à-Pitre?

F. sont des Départements d'Outre-Mer.

G. est dans la salle de classe.

H. es un membre de la famille.

15 Complete the crossword puzzle with either the appropriate subject pronoun or the appropriate form of the verb **être**.

Across

1. ... sont très intelligentes.
3. Tu n'... pas son frère.
5. Antoine... au cinéma.
7. ... êtes leur tante?
8. Je... au café.
10. ... est six heures.
11. Vous n'... pas sa mère.

Down

1. ... est délicieuse.
2. Nous... au fast-food.
4. ... ne sommes pas ses parents.
6. ... es timide.
9. Lucie et Guillaume... ensemble.
10. Ousmane et Cédric? ... sont en vacances.

16

Tell where the following people are by completing each sentence with the appropriate form of the verb **être**.

1. Je _________________________ à l'école.
2. Mes parents _________________________ en vacances.
3. Tu _________________________ avec qui?
4. Martine et moi, nous _________________________ à l'école.
5. Céline et Sandrine _________________________ au café avec leur frère.
6. Mon prof _________________________ à l'école.
7. Ma tante _________________________ au restaurant.
8. Et vous? Vous _________________________ où?

17

In the letter that follows, Amélie is writing about her friend Véronique's family. Complete Amélie's letter, using each of the listed words only once.

son	**sa**	**ses**	**leur**	**leurs**
ont	**est**	**sont**	**a**	

Sa mère _________________________ quarante ans et _________________________ père a quarante-trois ans. Sa mère _________________________ professeur de maths. _________________________ tante Irène a trente-quatre ans. Sa grand-mère et son grand-père sont _________________________ grands-parents. Ils _________________________ soixante-quatre ans. Ils _________________________ à Versailles, à dix-huit kilomètres de Paris. _________________________ chat et _________________________ chiens s'appellent Mistigris, Bruno et Médor.

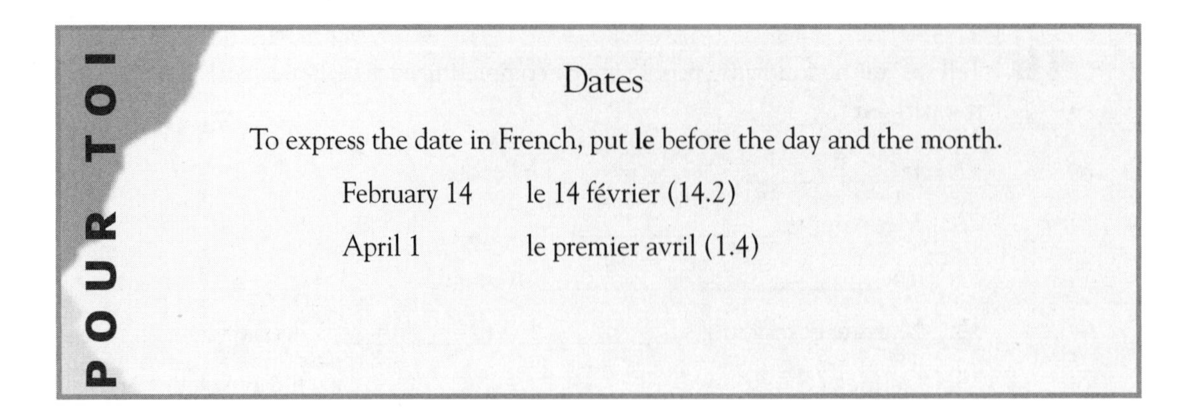

Dates

To express the date in French, put **le** before the day and the month.

February 14	le 14 février (14.2)
April 1	le premier avril (1.4)

18 Write each date in French.

1. January 8 ______________________
2. March 20 ______________________
3. November 11 ______________________
4. July 14 ______________________
5. October 30 ______________________
6. May 1 ______________________
7. June 5 ______________________
8. December 31 ______________________

19 Check your school's calendar to find out when some important days are this year. Then write the day of the week and the date of each one in French.

1. the first day of school

   ____

2. the first day of winter break

   ____

3. the first day back to school after winter break

   ____

4. the first day of spring break

   ____

5. the first day back to school after spring break

   ____

6. the last day of school

   ____

Leçon C

20

Match each English adjective with the letter of its French equivalent.

_____ 1.	shy, timid	A. beau, belle
_____ 2.	lazy	B. bête
_____ 3.	generous	C. sympa
_____ 4.	selfish	D. bavard(e)
_____ 5.	nice	E. intelligent(e)
_____ 6.	mean	F. égoïste
_____ 7.	talkative	G. timide
_____ 8.	handsome, beautiful	H. paresseux, paresseuse
_____ 9.	stupid, dumb	I. diligent(e)
_____ 10.	intelligent	J. généreux, généreuse
_____ 11.	hardworking	K. méchant(e)

21

Match each adjective with the letter of its opposite.

_____ 1.	égoïste	A. bête
_____ 2.	méchante	B. méchant
_____ 3.	diligent	C. bavard
_____ 4.	intelligente	D. diligente
_____ 5.	bête	E. sympa
_____ 6.	sympa	F. généreux
_____ 7.	paresseuse	G. paresseux
_____ 8.	timide	H. intelligent

22 Complete the crossword puzzle with the appropriate form of each indicated adjective.

Across

1. Antoinette est intelligente, et Antoine est... aussi.
6. Michel est paresseux, et Michèle est... aussi.
9. François est généreux, et Françoise est... aussi.
10. Christiane est diligente, et Christian est... aussi.
11. Patrick est bavard, et Patricia est... aussi.
12. Denis est égoïste, et Denise est... aussi.
13. Andrée est généreuse, et André est... aussi.

Down

2. Paul est intelligent, et Paulette est... aussi.
3. Amina est paresseuse, et Amine est... aussi.
4. Charlotte est bavarde, et Charles est... aussi.
5. René est diligent, et Renée est... aussi.
7. Jean est sympa, et Jeanne est... aussi.
8. Laurent est méchant, et Laurence est... aussi.

Agreement of adjectives

POUR TOI

Most masculine adjectives add an **e** to form the feminine.

un prof **bavard** une prof **bavarde**

Masculine adjectives that end in **-e** do not change in the feminine form.

un garçon **égoïste** une fille **égoïste**

Masculine adjectives that end in **-eux** have a feminine form that ends in **-euse**.

un étudiant **généreux** une étudiante **généreuse**

Most singular adjectives add an **s** to form the plural.

un chien **méchant** deux chiens **méchants**

The adjective **beau** has irregular forms.

un **beau** cousin un **bel** élève

une **belle** tante trois **beaux** cousins

23 Complete each sentence with the appropriate form of the indicated adjective.

1. (timide) Notre sœur est ________________.
2. (intelligent) Mes profs sont ________________.
3. (bête) Je ne suis pas ________________.
4. (beau) Ta grand-mère est ________________.
5. (bavard) Votre mère et votre sœur sont ________________.
6. (beau) Nos chats sont ________________.
7. (diligent) Leur cousine est ________________.
8. (généreux) Sa sœur est ________________.

24 Danièle has been thinking about the people she knows and has decided that everyone has an opposite. Say that the second person(s) mentioned is/are the opposite(s) of the first.

Modèle: Son père n'est pas bavard. Et sa mère?
Sa mère est bavarde.

1. Son frère n'est pas méchant. Et sa sœur?

____

2. Son grand-père est timide. Et sa grand-mère?

____

3. Sa tante est belle. Et son oncle?

____

4. Ses cousins ne sont pas bêtes. Et ses cousines?

____

5. Son prof de maths est paresseux. Et sa prof de chimie?

____

6. Ses parents ne sont pas généreux. Et ses grands-parents?

____

25 Write a description of three of your family members and three of your friends. Tell one characteristic that each person has and one characteristic that each one doesn't have. Finally, write two sentences about your qualities.

Modèle: *Ma mère est généreuse. Elle n'est pas égoïste.*
Chantal est sympa. Elle n'est pas méchante.

____

____

____

____

____

____

____

____

Unité 6 Tu viens d'où?

Leçon A

1 Based on where the following people are from, identify their nationality.

Modèle: Sophie est de Rome.
Elle est italienne.

1. Karl est de Berlin.
____
2. Luisa est de Mexico City.
____
3. Éric et Isabelle sont de Paris.
____
4. Liu (m.) est de Bejing.
____
5. Shirley et Dave sont de Londres.
____
6. Neil est de Toronto.
____
7. Ted et son frère sont de Cleveland.
____
8. José est de Madrid.
____
9. Sei (f.) et sa sœur sont de Tokyo.
____

2 Depending on each family's country of origin, tell their children's nationality.

Modèle: Les parents de Peter viennent d'Allemagne.
Il est allemand.

1. Les parents de Nathalie viennent de France.

____

2. Les parents de Sandra viennent d'Espagne.

____

3. Les parents de Tatsuo (m.) viennent du Japon.

____

4. Les parents de Susan et de James viennent du Canada.

____

5. Les parents de Felipe viennent du Mexique.

____

6. Les parents de Kati viennent de Chine.

____

7. Les parents de Sophia et de Carlo viennent d'Italie.

____

8. Les parents d'Élisabeth viennent d'Angleterre.

____

9. Les parents de Kai et de Thao (m.) viennent du Vietnam.

____

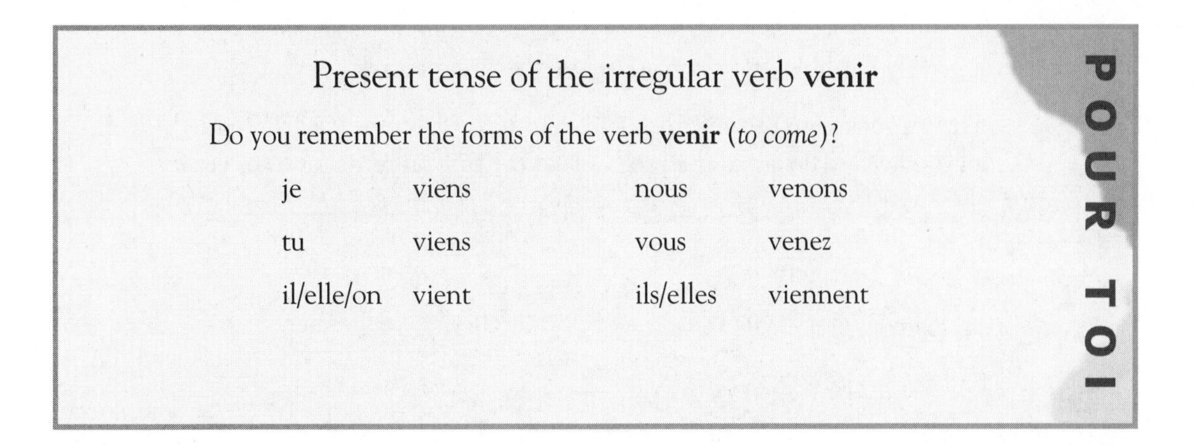

POUR TOI

Present tense of the irregular verb **venir**

Do you remember the forms of the verb **venir** (*to come*)?

je	viens	nous	venons
tu	viens	vous	venez
il/elle/on	vient	ils/elles	viennent

3 Complete the crossword puzzle with either the appropriate subject pronoun or the appropriate form of the verb **venir**.

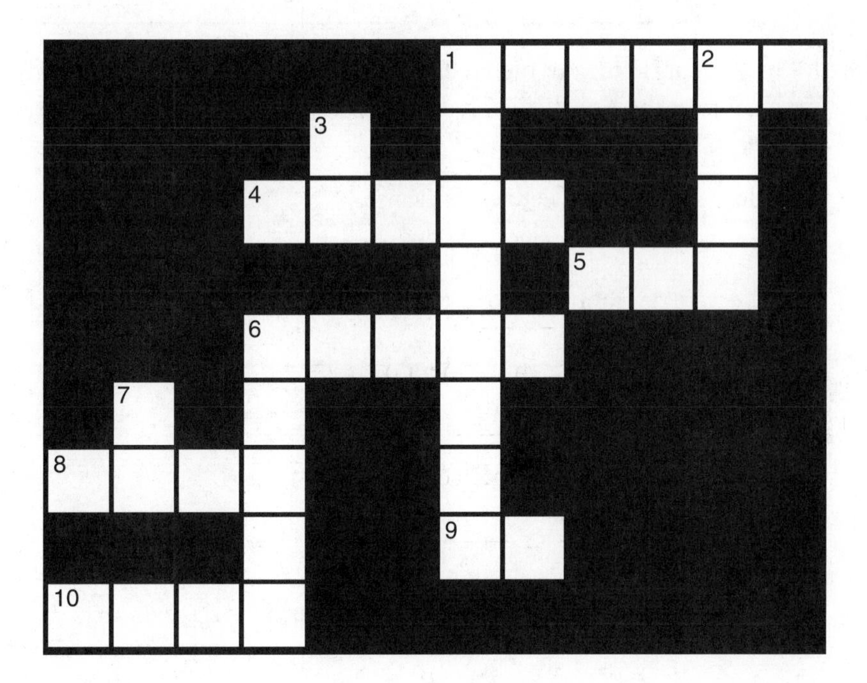

Across

1. Nous... à huit heures.
4. Est-ce que vous... avec vos parents?
5. Non,... ne viennent pas.
6. Il... avec sa sœur.
8. Patricia? Est-ce qu'... vient?
9. À quelle heure est-ce que... viens?
10. Alors,... venez à sept heures?

Down

1. Paul et son frère... ensemble.
2. ... ne venons pas demain.
3. Moi,... viens d'Angleterre.
6. Et toi? Tu... avec ton cousin?
7. Mon prof? ... ne vient pas.

POUR TOI

Revenir: another verb like **venir**

The irregular verb **revenir** means "to return" or "to come back." To use this verb, all you need to do is add the prefix **re-** to the present tense forms of **venir**.

je	reviens	nous	revenons
tu	reviens	vous	revenez
il/elle/on	revient	ils/elles	reviennent

De + definite articles

Do you remember how **de** combines with **le** and **les**?

de + le = du
de + les = des

4 Many students from your high school are foreign exchange students this year. Knowing the nationality of these exchange students' host sister(s) or brother(s), tell what country each American student is coming back from.

Modèle: La sœur de Clark est française.
Il revient de France.

1. Le frère de Jeannie est japonais.

____

2. Nos frères sont allemands.

____

3. Ta sœur est mexicaine.

____

4. Le frère de Peggy et de Pauline est espagnol.

____

5. La sœur de Xai (m.) est canadienne.

____

6. Mes frères et ma sœur sont chinois.

____

7. Vos sœurs sont françaises.

____

8. Les sœurs de Robbie et de Kevin sont italiennes.

____

5 Your French teacher has a collection of items that have been left in class. Tell whom they belong to.

Modèles: le cahier/l'étudiante avec les cheveux blonds
C'est le cahier de l'étudiante avec les cheveux blonds.

les cassettes/le cousin de Paul
Ce sont les cassettes du cousin de Paul.

1. le stylo/l'élève qui étudie l'espagnol
C'est le stylo du l'élève qui étudie l'espagnol

2. le sac à dos/la fille avec les yeux bleus
C'est le sac à dos de la fille avec les yeux bleus

3. les crayons/les garçons qui jouent au basket
Ce sont le crayons du le garçons qui jouent au basket

4. le CD/la sœur de Bertrand
C'est le ~~DD~~ CD de la soeur de Bertrand

5. le livre de français/l'étudiant qui n'étudie pas
C'est le ~~livre~~ livre de français du l'étudiant qui n'étudie pas.

6. la trousse/le frère de Bruno
C'est la trousse du le frère du Bruno

7. le dictionnaire/la cousine de Yasmine
C'est le dictionnaire de la cousine de Yasmine

8. les vidéocassettes/les professeurs
~~C'est le~~ Ce sont les vidéocassettes du les professeurs.

6 During his year in France, Jerry was asked to interview teachers and students from his French school who had spent their summer vacations in various countries. Rewrite his notes, using complete questions and answers. (The first two sets have been done for you.)

1. Mme Verley? (Canada)
2. Damien? (Chine)
3. Théo? (Angleterre)
4. M. Cousseman? (Japon)
5. Zakia? (Espagne)
6. Mlle Clech? (Vietnam)
7. M. et Mme Okada? (Allemagne)
8. Nadia et Mohamed? (Italie)
9. Yasmine? (Mexique)
10. Mme Torti? (États-Unis)

1. *D'où revenez-vous?*
   Je reviens du Canada.
2. *D'où reviens-tu?*
   Je reviens de Chine.
3. D'où reviend-tu?
   Je reviens du Angleterre.
4. D'où revenez vous?
   Je reviens du Japon.
5. D'où reviens-tu?
   Je reviens de Espagne
6. D'où revenez-vous?
   Je reviens du Vietname
7. D'où revennons-nous?
   Nous revennons de Allemagne.
8. D'où revenez-vous?
   Je revenez de Italie.
9. D'où reviens-tu?
   Je reviens du Mexique
10. D'où ~~reve~~ revenez-vous?
    Je reviens de États-Unis.

Forming questions

POUR TOI

There are three basic ways to ask a question that can be answered by "yes" or "no":

1. Make your tone of voice rise at the end of a sentence.
2. Put **est-ce que** before the subject.
3. Put **n'est-ce pas** at the end of a sentence.

7 Students at the International Festival tell what countries they come from. Now ask them if their nationality corresponds to that country.

Modèle: Robert: "Je viens d'Angleterre."
Est-ce que tu es anglais?

1. Sarah: "Je viens du Canada."
Est-ce que tu es canadien?
2. Marta: "Je viens d'Espagne."
Est-ce que tu es espagnol?
3. Pedro: "Je viens du Mexique."
Est-ce que tu es mexicain?
4. Michael: "Je viens de Chine."
Est-ce que tu es chinoise?
5. Michiko (f.): "Je viens du Japon."
Est-ce que tu es japonese?
6. Nathalie: "Je viens de France."
Est-ce que tu es français?
7. Hans: "Je viens d'Allemagne."
Est-ce que tu es allemand?
8. Bénédicte (f.): "Je viens d'Italie."
Est-ce que tu es italien?

8 Match the question with the letter of the appropriate answer.

_____ 1. Pourquoi est-ce que tu étudies le français?
_____ 2. Tu viens d'où?
_____ 3. Comment est-ce que le prof skie?
_____ 4. Où est-ce que tu vas?
_____ 5. Les crêpes coûtent combien?
_____ 6. Vous allez à l'école, n'est-ce pas?
_____ 7. Avec qui est-ce que tu joues au foot?
_____ 8. Tu es le professeur?

A. Très bien.
B. Deux euros vingt-neuf.
C. Ma sœur.
D. Parce que j'ai des parents à Paris.
E. Non.
F. Au Canada.
G. Des États-Unis.
H. Oui.

9 Serge, a visiting student from Belgium, is coming to your French class. Rearrange the following words, forming questions you could ask him.

1. t'appelles/est-ce que/tu/comment

____

2. es/pourquoi/tu/États-Unis/est-ce que/aux (*in the*)

____

3. tu/d'où/viens/est-ce que

____

4. français/es/est-ce que/tu

____

5. membres/sont/famille/de/qui/ta/les

____

6. à/ressembles/père/tu/ton

____

7. l'école/où/vas/est-ce que/tu/à

____

8. est-ce que/au/tu/avec/cinéma/vas/qui

____

Leçon B

10 Find and circle the names of 16 professions in French.

V	R	E	I	N	I	S	I	U	C	R	D	J	H	B
K	K	W	N	R	E	L	B	A	T	P	M	O	C	V
X	E	H	F	E	N	I	C	E	D	É	M	U	G	I
I	C	U	O	I	K	Q	U	V	K	M	R	R	N	H
B	I	Q	R	M	M	X	I	E	E	L	U	N	W	G
K	L	W	M	R	M	G	Z	D	D	E	E	A	V	P
D	O	Q	A	E	V	E	A	T	I	S	F	L	Q	O
Q	P	X	T	F	V	F	A	N	V	P	F	I	C	J
T	E	B	I	L	F	J	É	U	W	S	I	S	Z	K
G	D	I	C	A	Y	G	B	N	F	A	O	T	W	H
E	T	S	I	T	N	E	D	A	F	O	C	E	L	B
E	N	R	E	I	M	R	I	F	N	I	Y	G	S	O
L	E	W	N	M	P	R	O	F	E	S	S	E	U	R
S	G	A	D	C	J	W	S	E	R	V	E	U	R	U
T	A	C	O	V	A	M	T	N	Y	O	P	Q	A	Y

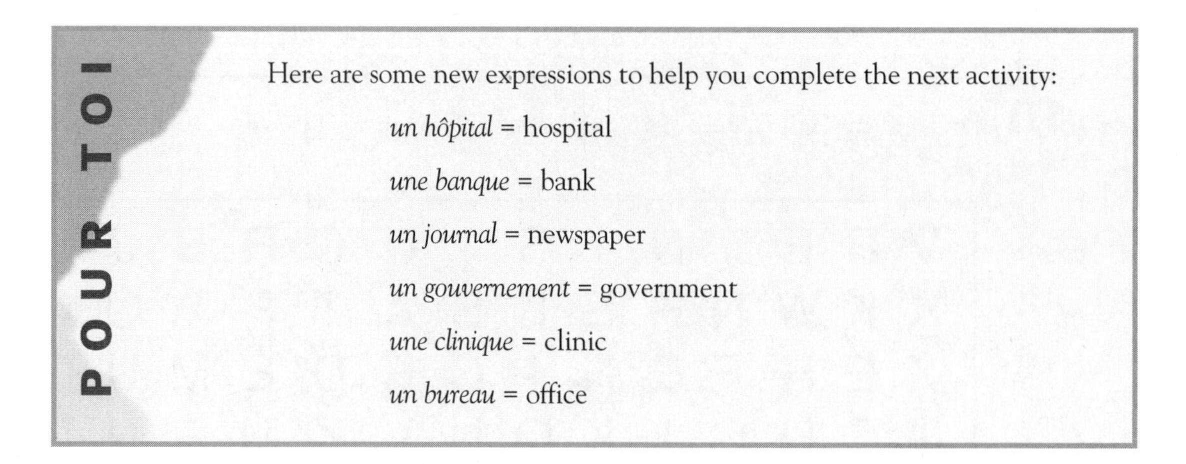

Here are some new expressions to help you complete the next activity:

un hôpital = hospital

une banque = bank

un journal = newspaper

un gouvernement = government

une clinique = clinic

un bureau = office

11 Your classmates give you clues to help you guess what their parents do. For each person described, make two logical guesses.

Modèle: Ma mère travaille dans un hôpital.
Est-ce qu'elle est médecin ou infirmière?

1. Mon père travaille dans une banque.

 ____

2. Ma mère travaille pour un journal.

 ____

3. Ma mère travaille dans un café.

 ____

4. Mon père travaille pour le gouvernement.

 ____

5. Mon père travaille dans une clinique.

 ____

6. Ma mère travaille dans une école.

 ____

7. Ma mère travaille dans un bureau.

 ____

Indefinite articles in negative sentences

POUR TOI

The words **un**, **une** and **des** change to **de** or **d'** in a negative sentence.

Tu as **des** disquettes? Non, je n'ai pas **de** disquettes.

12 Say that none of the students has the school supplies the teacher had requested.

Modèle: Odile/des crayons
Elle n'a pas de crayons.

1. Djamel et Marc/un dictionnaire

____

2. Céline/une trousse

____

3. Vincent/un sac à dos

____

4. Assia et Khadim/des stylos

____

5. Gilberte/un livre de français

____

6. Martine et Alain/des feuilles de papier

____

7. Édouard/une cassette

____

8. Normand et Hervé/une disquette

____

13 Answer the following questions about your family.

Modèle: Est-ce que tu as des frères?
Oui, j'ai des frères. ou
Non, je n'ai pas de frères.

1. Est-ce que tu as une tante française?
____
2. Est-ce que tu as des demi-frères?
____
3. Est-ce que tu as un grand-père italien?
____
4. Est-ce que tu as des belles-sœurs?
____
5. Est-ce que tu as une sœur?
____
6. Est-ce que tu as des cousins allemands?
____
7. Est-ce que tu as un beau-père?
____
8. Est-ce que tu as une belle-mère?
____

The interrogative adjective **quel**

POUR TOI

Here are the forms of the adjective **quel**:

	Masculine	**Feminine**
Singular	quel	quelle
Plural	quels	quelles

14 Your teacher asks for your help in trying to find some classroom objects. You ask your teacher to be more specific.

Modèle: Le dictionnaire?
Quel dictionnaire?

1. Le magnétoscope? ______
2. Les cassettes françaises? ______
3. Les CDs? ______
4. Les stylos noirs? ______
5. Le calendrier? ______
6. La disquette? ______
7. Le cahier gris? ______
8. Les vidéocassettes? ______

15 A local veterinarian is from Montréal. As part of a school project, Antoine would like to interview him in French. How should he ask the veterinarian each of the following questions?

Modèle: What goldfish do you like?
Quels poissons rouges est-ce que vous aimez?

1. What days do you work?
______
2. What hours do you work?
______
3. What computer do you have?
______

4. What cats are mean?

____

5. What dogs are intelligent?

____

6. What bird is nice?

____

7. What horse do you prefer?

____

8. What music do you like?

____

POUR TOI

C'est vs. il/elle est

Il est or **Elle est** is used when the next word is an adjective or the name of a nationality or an occupation.

Elle est généreuse. **Il est** italien. **Elle est** cuisinière.

C'est is used when the noun that follows is modified by an article, an adjective or both.

C'est un professeur. **C'est** mon frère. **C'est** une bonne avocate.

16 Describe your foreign acquaintances by using **il est**, **elle est** or **c'est**. You may also need to use the corresponding plural forms.

Modèle: Catherine parle français. *Elle est* sympa. *C'est* une Canadienne.

1. Brigit est allemande. _______________ une fille paresseuse. _______________ égoïste.
2. Magali est de Casablanca. _______________ timide, et _______________ infirmière.
3. Carlos n'est pas français. _______________ un garçon bavard. _______________ diligent aussi.
4. Pierre et Jacques sont canadiens. _______________ méchants! _______________ des garçons bêtes.

5. Charles et Daniel sont de Genève. ______________________ des garçons sympa.
   ______________________ généreux.
6. Karl est de Berlin. ______________________ allemand.
   ______________________ un beau garçon, mais ______________ timide.
7. Anne et Myriam sont les sœurs de Jean-Paul. ______________________
   bavardes. ______________________ des filles blondes.
8. Sonia et Florence sont des filles intelligentes. ______________________
   françaises, et ______________________ belles.

17 Choose three of your friends and then write three sentences about each of them. Identify your friend in the first sentence. Begin the second sentence with **C'est**. Start the final sentence with **Il est** or **Elle est**.

Modèle: *Il s'appelle Mark. C'est un garçon sympa. Il est bavard.*

____

____

____

____

____

____

____

____

____

____

____

____

Leçon C

18

Unscramble the seasonal weather descriptions that follow. Begin each sentence with the name of the season.

Modèle: printemps/mauvais/fait/il/au
Au printemps il fait mauvais.

1. hiver/fait/en/il/froid

 ____

2. pleut/en/il/automne

 ____

3. fait/été/soleil/il/en/du

 ____

4. printemps/au/fait/beau/il

 ____

5. neige/il/hiver/en

 ____

6. chaud/fait/été/il/en

 ____

7. automne/frais/il/en/fait

 ____

8. fait/au/vent/du/printemps/il

 ____

19 Assia received postcards from people who were traveling in various parts of the world. Describe the weather in each postcard by using two different weather expressions.

____

____

____

____

____

____

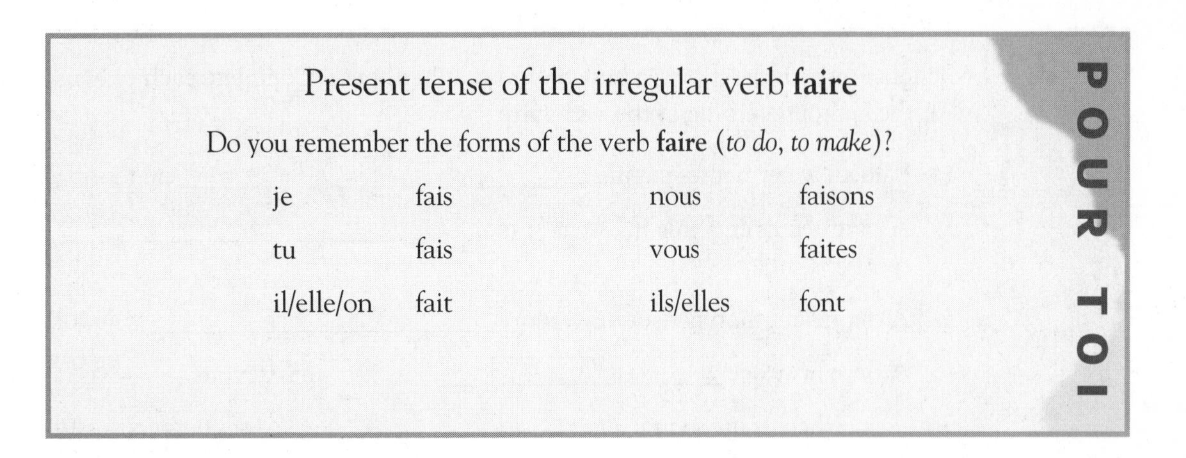

Present tense of the irregular verb **faire**

Do you remember the forms of the verb **faire** (*to do, to make*)?

je	fais	nous	faisons
tu	fais	vous	faites
il/elle/on	fait	ils/elles	font

POUR TOI

20 Complete the crossword puzzle with either the appropriate subject pronoun or the appropriate form of the verb **faire**.

Across

1. ... fais du footing.
3. Jean et toi, vous... du roller.
4. ... fait mauvais.
5. Il... du soleil.
7. Renée et Amina,... font des crêpes.
9. ... faisons un tour.
10. Quel sport est-ce que... faites?
11. ... ne fais pas de sport?

Down

2. ... fait une omelette.
3. Nous... du shopping.
5. Qu'est-ce que tu...?
6. ... font du vélo.
8. Les élèves... les devoirs.

21 Michèle Poitras is describing a busy Saturday at her house. Complete each of her sentences with the appropriate form of the verb **faire**.

1. Samedi à sept heures ma mère ______________________________ du footing.
2. À huit heures et demie ma sœur et moi, nous ______________________________ du sport ensemble.
3. À dix heures mon père et ma sœur ______________________________ du roller.
4. À onze heures je ______________________________ mes devoirs.
5. À onze heures ma sœur ______________________________ ses devoirs aussi.
6. À midi nous ______________________________ une salade et des sandwichs.
7. À deux heures mes parents ______________________________ un tour ensemble.
8. Et vous? Qu'est-ce que vous ________________?

22 Frédéric is an exchange student from Switzerland. He's writing a story about American teenagers for his hometown newspaper. Answer his questions.

1. Qu'est-ce que tu fais à l'école?

   ____

2. Qu'est-ce que tu fais après les cours?

   ____

3. Qu'est-ce que tu fais le samedi avec tes amis?

   ____

4. Qu'est-ce que tu fais comme sport?

   ____

5. Est-ce que tu fais du sport avec tes amis ou avec ta famille?

   ____

6. Où est-ce que tu fais du shopping? Avec qui?

   ____

7. Qu'est-ce que tu fais en vacances?

   ____

8. Qu'est-ce que tes parents font quand ils travaillent?

   ____

Forming questions with inversion

POUR TOI

To ask a question with inversion, the order is:

verb + subject pronoun

If the subject of the sentence is a noun, add the appropriate subject pronoun after the verb.

Mme Lenore fait-**elle** du shopping?

If the **il, elle** or **on** form of the verb ends with a vowel, add **-t-** between the verb and its subject pronoun.

A-**t**-il une sœur?

23 Now switch roles with Frédéric in Activity 22. So that you can prepare an article for your school newspaper about life in Switzerland, form questions using inversion to ask him.

Modèle: tu/étudier l'anglais
Étudies-tu l'anglais?

1. tes amis/parler anglais

____

2. tes amis et toi/regarder la télé après les cours

____

3. tes amis/aimer aller au cinéma

____

4. tes parents/travailler beaucoup

____

5. ton père/être ingénieur

____

6. ta famille et toi/faire du vélo

____

7. ton frère/aller souvent au fast-food

____

8. ta sœur/nager

____

24 Your classmate has written a series of answers. For each one write the inverted question you would need to ask to get that specific answer.

Modèle: Je viens à l'école avec ma sœur.
Avec qui viens-tu à l'école?

1. J'ai quatorze ans.

 ____

2. J'arrive à l'école à sept heures et demie.

 ____

3. J'aime mes professeurs.

 ____

4. Je préfère le français.

 ____

5. À midi nous mangeons au fast-food.

 ____

6. Je regarde la télé à huit heures.

 ____

7. Je téléphone à mon amie Suzanne.

 ____

8. Je fais du shopping le samedi.

 ____

Unité 7 On fait les magasins.

Leçon A

1 Unscramble the following items of clothing and types of stores. Add **un** or **une** to each word, as appropriate.

1. nnataolp
   pantaloa
2. nigmsaa
   magasin
3. rknoaa
   anorak
4. uooslnb
   blouson
5. tubeiquo
   boutique
6. mnslbeee
   ensemble
7. suetcmo
   costume
8. ltmloia
   maillot
9. mhsciee
   chemise
10. phacuae
    chapeau

2 Find and circle the names of 24 items of clothing in French.

M	B	Y	L	M	J	W	Q	C	D	P	U	O	S	U
R	A	L	N	T	E	E	S	H	I	R	T	U	I	L
V	U	I	O	N	A	O	M	A	P	Y	E	N	R	B
P	E	E	L	U	N	E	R	U	E	L	L	I	A	T
D	X	S	A	L	S	S	N	S	T	E	K	S	A	B
U	K	I	T	T	O	O	H	S	X	S	E	B	O	R
P	A	M	N	E	R	T	N	U	E	T	O	H	T	I
G	R	E	A	W	E	O	D	R	T	M	C	C	S	Q
Q	O	H	P	N	X	N	H	E	R	Z	B	W	E	Q
Z	N	C	N	A	H	V	S	S	B	O	E	L	S	S
O	A	I	I	R	H	S	N	C	U	A	V	R	E	M
K	S	A	A	X	U	C	Q	H	T	U	I	P	T	O
S	M	G	U	A	E	T	N	A	M	F	U	N	T	L
O	V	W	H	L	V	U	I	G	U	J	E	F	O	Y
S	I	C	P	M	L	U	E	C	E	L	T	O	B	D

3 Imagine that you were on a TV game show and won five hundred dollars to go on a shopping spree. List the items that you would buy at each place. Also give each item's price.

une boutique	un grand magasin	un centre commercial

4 Imagine that you have been chosen to spend the next school year in Nice, France. Prepare your packing list, remembering that you can go skiing in the Alps in the winter and swimming in the Mediterranean Sea in early fall and late spring. Don't forget to add clothing for school and more formal occasions as well.

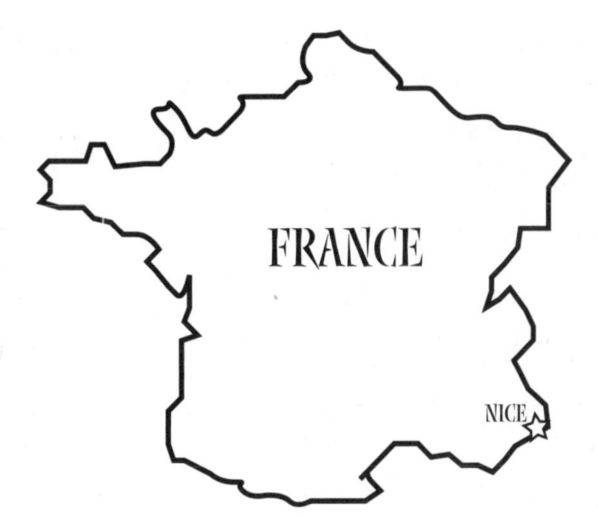

l'automne	l'hiver	le printemps
tee-shirt	pantalon	un shorts
jupe	pull	un sandals
un jean	anorak	un camise
un chemise	blouson	un malliot de bain
un vest	manteau	des tennis
des tennis	bottes	des baskets
des basket	bas	une [illegible]
des chaussure	vest	des chaussure

POUR TOI

Aller + infinitive

To express what you are going to do in the near future, use:

present tense form of **aller** + infinitive

Je **vais jouer** au basket. *I'm going to play basketball.*

5 What we have often indicates what we are going to do. Read what the following people have and then write what they are going to do.

Modèle: J'ai ma raquette.
Je vais jouer au tennis.

1. Tu as ton vélo.

   ____

2. Nous avons nos livres, nos cahiers et nos stylos.

   ____

3. J'ai des crêpes.

   ____

4. Caroline a ses skis.

   ____

5. M. et Mme Blondel ont cent cinquante euros.

   ____

6. Vous avez vos CDs.

   ____

7. Frédéric a son maillot de bain.

   ____

8. Valérie et Gilberte ont une vidéocassette.

   ____

6 Since it's a beautiful day, people are going to take advantage of the weather. Of the two activities, say that people are going to do the one that is usually done outside.

Modèle: Mme Duria aime faire du shopping, et elle aime nager.
Elle va nager.

1. M. Fertey aime travailler à la banque, et il aime faire du footing.

 ____

2. Nous aimons jouer au basket, et nous aimons écouter de la musique.

 ____

3. Tu aimes faire du sport, et tu aimes lire.

 ____

4. Ariane aime téléphoner, et elle aime sortir.

 ____

5. Vous aimez jouer au volley, et vous aimez regarder la télé.

 ____

6. Hervé et Sonia aiment jouer aux jeux vidéo, et ils aiment faire un tour.

 ____

7. J'aime étudier, et j'aime faire du roller.

 ____

8. Françoise et Stéphanie aiment faire les devoirs, et elles aiment jouer au foot.

 ____

7 It's the week of semester exams, so everyone's schedule is different. Say that the following students are studying and are not going to take part in their favorite activities.

Modèle: Khaled aime faire du roller.
Il étudie. Il ne va pas faire du roller.

1. Vous aimez jouer aux jeux vidéo.

 ____

2. Christophe aime faire du vélo.

 ____

3. Tu aimes écouter la radio.

 ____

4. Laurent et Malick aiment regarder la télé.

 ____

5. Nous aimons faire du footing.

 ____

6. Myriam et Jeanne aiment aller au cinéma.

 ____

7. Béatrice aime faire du shopping.

 ____

8. J'aime aller au fast-food.

 ____

8 Answer the following questions.

Modèle: Vas-tu manger au fast-food ou à la cantine aujourd'hui?
Je vais manger à la cantine aujourd'hui.

1. Qu'est-ce que tu vas manger?

   ____

2. Vas-tu étudier le français ou l'anglais pour demain?

   ____

3. Vas-tu porter un jean ou un pantalon demain?

   ____

4. Est-ce que tu vas parler français avec ton professeur demain?

   ____

5. Qu'est-ce que tu vas faire samedi?

   ____

6. Où est-ce que tu vas voyager un jour? En France? En Angleterre?

   ____

7. Est-ce que tu vas skier en France un jour?

   ____

8. Qu'est-ce que tu vas être? Un professeur de français?

   ____

POUR TOI

À + definite articles

Do you remember how **à** combines with **le** and **les**?

à + le = **au**

à + les = **aux**

9 To say where the following people are going tomorrow, complete the sentences with **à la**, **à l'**, **au** or **aux**.

1. M. Verchère va voyager __________________ Mexique.
2. Les élèves vont manger __________________ fast-food.
3. Mme Hamel va __________________ Guadeloupe.
4. Nous allons faire du shopping __________________ grands magasins.
5. Vous allez étudier ______________ école.
6. Mme Poirier et Mlle Rochet vont aller __________________ États-Unis.

10 Everyone is looking for something or someone. Tell where people are looking by choosing the most appropriate location from the list. Then write **à la**, **à l'**, **au** or **aux** before your choice. Use each location only once.

fast-food	café	GRAND MAGASIN	CANTINE
école	boum	magasin	centre commercial

Modèle: Mme Kidjo cherche une robe *à la boutique*.

1. Jeanne et Marie cherchent des bas ______________________________.
2. M. Caprioli cherche un costume ______________________________.
3. Nous cherchons nos amis ______________________________.
4. Charles et Éric cherchent leur professeur de français ______________________________.
5. Tu cherches une pizza et un coca ______________________________.
6. Mme Ferras cherche des disquettes ______________________________.
7. Je cherche un hamburger, des frites et une limonade ______________________________.
8. Vous cherchez un sandwich au jambon et un jus d'orange ______________________________.

Leçon B

11

Find and circle the feminine names of 12 colors in French.

V	E	R	T	E	G	U	O	R	F	E	V	Q	T	E
K	I	L	Z	K	N	P	T	E	A	G	M	H	U	R
X	N	O	R	R	A	M	H	N	T	I	H	E	Z	I
M	A	O	L	Q	K	E	Z	U	T	E	L	S	J	O
F	B	A	E	E	H	C	N	A	L	B	X	O	E	N
I	G	K	M	Y	T	L	G	J	U	W	F	R	R	X
P	K	O	A	N	K	T	U	W	W	O	D	Q	W	N
L	U	I	D	W	Z	S	E	R	Q	N	K	R	O	F
C	S	W	S	V	U	L	R	G	U	D	W	M	L	Y
Y	E	Z	W	K	Z	K	F	R	N	T	I	F	F	Y
Z	M	J	L	D	U	L	T	I	V	A	V	J	A	N
M	I	G	C	E	B	F	U	S	K	O	R	Y	P	Y
N	O	I	E	J	C	C	E	E	V	O	L	O	V	J

12

Match each adjective with the letter of its opposite.

_____ 1. nouveau
_____ 2. bon marché
_____ 3. petit
_____ 4. court
_____ 5. joli
_____ 6. vieille
_____ 7. grande
_____ 8. longue

A. grand
B. nouvelle
C. cher
D. petite
E. long
F. courte
G. vieux
H. moche

POUR TOI

Irregular adjectives

Some masculine adjectives double the final consonant and add an **e** to form the feminine.

un magasin **canadien**	une boutique **canadienne**

Masculine adjectives that end in **-er** change the ending to **-ère** to form the feminine.

un short **cher**	une robe **chère**

Some masculine adjectives have irregular feminine forms.

un chapeau **blanc**	une chemise **blanche**
un sandwich **frais**	une boisson **fraîche**
un pantalon **long**	une jupe **longue**

Some adjectives never change form, even in the plural.

orange

marron

super

sympa

bon marché

Three adjectives have irregular feminine forms and irregular forms before a masculine noun beginning with a vowel sound.

un **beau** chien	un **bel** oiseau	une **belle** jupe
un **nouveau** tailleur	un **nouvel** ami	une **nouvelle** chemise
un **vieux** costume	un **vieil** ensemble	une **vieille** robe

13 Circle the feminine forms of the 14 masculine adjectives listed below.

W	Z	D	W	B	J	B	V	I	O	L	E	T	T	E
N	E	I	T	V	V	I	T	U	T	H	B	K	N	F
O	G	R	I	S	E	A	C	R	C	U	B	U	C	F
U	N	O	È	I	L	B	O	N	N	E	A	J	O	J
V	E	I	L	I	Y	O	A	Q	D	J	D	X	M	O
E	O	L	E	K	M	L	N	O	I	R	E	I	V	G
L	E	N	L	X	B	E	F	G	V	F	E	C	O	P
L	N	G	R	E	S	J	R	L	U	C	W	K	F	U
E	Y	N	F	Q	U	S	A	P	B	E	L	L	E	R
F	Q	Y	D	V	C	Q	Î	C	F	E	Q	M	Z	S
U	V	T	W	R	B	T	C	P	A	Q	W	R	T	L
Q	Y	Z	K	T	O	N	H	O	Y	X	E	Q	J	R
R	P	W	Z	E	F	C	E	J	E	S	G	Z	I	U

1. gris
2. bon
3. long
4. vieux
5. violet
6. noir
7. premier
8. blanc
9. quel
10. italien
11. beau
12. jaune
13. nouveau
14. frais

14 Complete the following sentences with the appropriate form of the indicated adjective.

1. (gris) Henri a un costume ____________________.
2. (rouge) Mme Doucette porte une chemise ____________________.
3. (bon) J'ai un ____________________ livre de français.
4. (mauvais) C'est une ____________________ étudiante.
5. (frais) Sa mère fait une salade ____________________.

6. (vietnamien) Leur belle-mère est ______________________.
7. (premier) C'est ma ______________________ boum.
8. (moche) Ton chien n'est pas ______________________.
9. (grand) Mme Dumont est très ______________________.
10. (blanc) Ma nouvelle jupe est ______________________.
11. (espagnol) Pedro parle à son amie ______________________.
12. (court) Sylvie porte une robe ______________________.
13. (orange) Michel a des chaussures ______________________.
14. (beau) Oh là là! C'est un ______________________ homme.
15. (allemand) Ma grand-mère est ______________________.

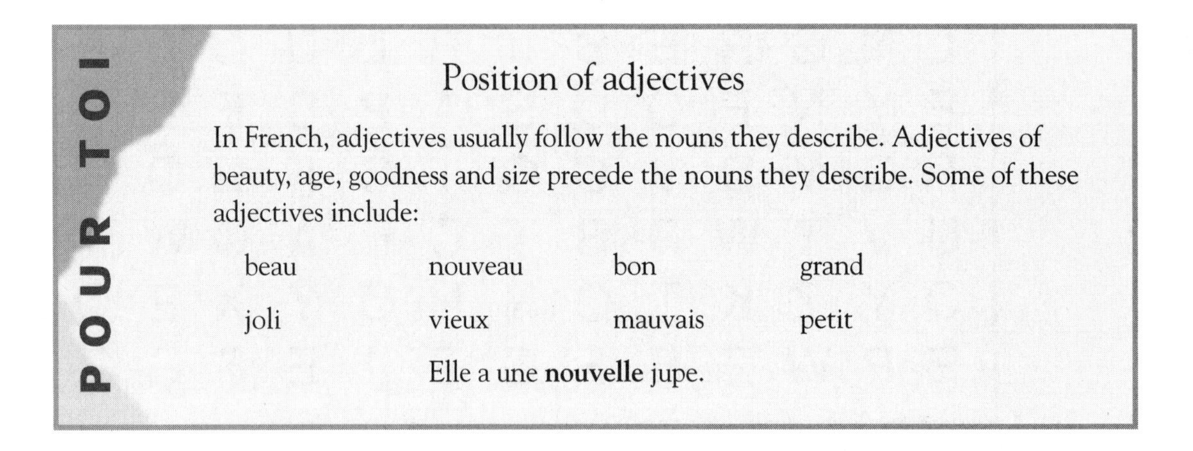

POUR TOI

Position of adjectives

In French, adjectives usually follow the nouns they describe. Adjectives of beauty, age, goodness and size precede the nouns they describe. Some of these adjectives include:

beau	nouveau	bon	grand
joli	vieux	mauvais	petit

Elle a une **nouvelle** jupe.

15 Rewrite each of the following sentences, adding the correct form of the indicated adjective.

Modèle: J'ai besoin d'une chemise. (nouveau)
J'ai besoin d'une nouvelle chemise.

1. Marc et Céline ont deux vélos. (petit)

____

2. M. Djibouti adore la musique. (américain)

____

3. On passe un film au Gaumont. (bon)

____

4. Notre professeur de sciences porte un costume. (vieux)

____

5. Donnez-moi une boisson, s'il vous plaît. (frais)

6. Je voudrais une glace. (italien)

7. Oh là là! C'est une boutique! (grand)

8. Paul va acheter un jean. (noir)

16 At the café Jean-François is describing everything his family has ordered. Rearrange the words to form logical sentences.

1. desserts/cousines/deux/mes/jolis/ont

2. père/petites/mon/crêpes/a/deux

3. steak-frites/bon/sœur/ma/a/un

4. frais/d'orange/mère/a/ma/jus/un

5. pommes/oncle/a/belle/mon/une/aux/tarte

6. sandwich/ma/un/grand-mère/chaud/a

7. espagnole/mon/grand-père/une/a/omelette

8. grande/ai/une/glace/j'/au chocolat

17 Write a paragraph about eight things you own. Use two adjectives to describe each item. You may want to refer to the following lists of possible adjectives and nouns to give you some ideas.

Adjectives

petit	grand	nouveau	vieux
bon	mauvais	beau	joli
français	américain	anglais	italien
blanc	noir	vert	rouge

Nouns

un anorak	un blouson	un jean	une chemise
des chaussures	un chat	un chien	un ensemble
un pull	un sweat	un crayon	un CD
une télé	un vélo	un ordinateur	un sac à dos

Modèle: *J'ai un bon vélo américain.*

Present tense of the verbs **acheter** and **préférer**

POUR TOI

Note the accent marks on certain forms of the verbs **acheter** (*to buy*) and **préférer** (*to prefer*).

j'	achète	nous	achetons
tu	achètes	vous	achetez
il/elle/on	achète	ils/elles	achètent

je	préfère	nous	préférons
tu	préfères	vous	préférez
il/elle/on	préfère	ils/elles	préfèrent

18 Weekend sales have drawn a crowd to Paris' largest shopping center. Say what everyone is buying, using the verb **acheter**.

1. Mme Hulot ____________________ une nouvelle robe rose.
2. Nous ____________________ des CDs américains.
3. J'____________________ une vieille cassette de Johnny Hallyday.
4. André et Antoine ____________________ des baskets.
5. Tu ____________________ un ordinateur et des disquettes.
6. M. Renaud ____________________ un nouveau costume gris.
7. Vous ____________________ un pull vert et un pantalon beige.

19 Saturday it's raining, so no one is going out. Tell what everyone prefers doing at home, using the verb **préférer**.

1. Nous ____________________ écouter de la musique.
2. M. et Mme Bernaise ____________________ regarder la télé.
3. Alicia ____________________ étudier les maths.
4. Bertrand et son beau-frère ____________________ jouer aux jeux vidéos.
5. Vous ____________________ faire les devoirs.
6. Tu ____________________ lire un livre en français.
7. Je ____________________ dormir.

Leçon C

20

To compare sizes in France and the United States, look at the chart on page 241 of your textbook. Then give the French equivalent of the following American sizes.

Modèle: Pour acheter une robe, Sue fait du huit aux États-Unis.
En France, elle fait du trente-six.

1. Pour acheter un pantalon, Jeff fait du trente-sept aux États-Unis.

 ____

2. Pour acheter un pull, Kaitlyn fait du quatorze aux États-Unis.

 ____

3. Pour acheter une chemise, Randy fait du seize aux États-Unis.

 ____

4. Pour acheter des bas, Tricia fait du neuf aux États-Unis.

 ____

5. Pour acheter une robe, Jenny fait du douze aux États-Unis.

 ____

6. Pour acheter un costume, Rich fait du quarante-deux aux États-Unis.

 ____

7. Pour acheter un pull, Mike fait du quarante-six aux États-Unis.

 ____

8. Pour acheter des chaussures, Dan fait du dix aux États-Unis.

 ____

21 Complete the conversation that follows, using each of the listed words only once.

centre	taille	vais	combien
fais	vendeur	acheter	VIENS

THÉRÈSE: Tu vas ________________________ un nouveau pantalon aujourd'hui?

JACQUES: Oui, je vais au ________________________ commercial. Tu ________________________?

THÉRÈSE: D'accord. Quelle ________________________ fais-tu? Je ________________________ du 38.

JACQUES: Moi, je fais du 42. Je ________________________ acheter des bottes aussi.

au magasin

THÉRÈSE: Voilà le ________________________!

LE VENDEUR: Oui, Monsieur? Un pantalon?

JACQUES: Oui, je fais du 42. Je cherche un pantalon beige.

LE VENDEUR: Ah... voilà un 42 en beige.

JACQUES: C'est ________________________, Monsieur?

LE VENDEUR: 45,58 euros.

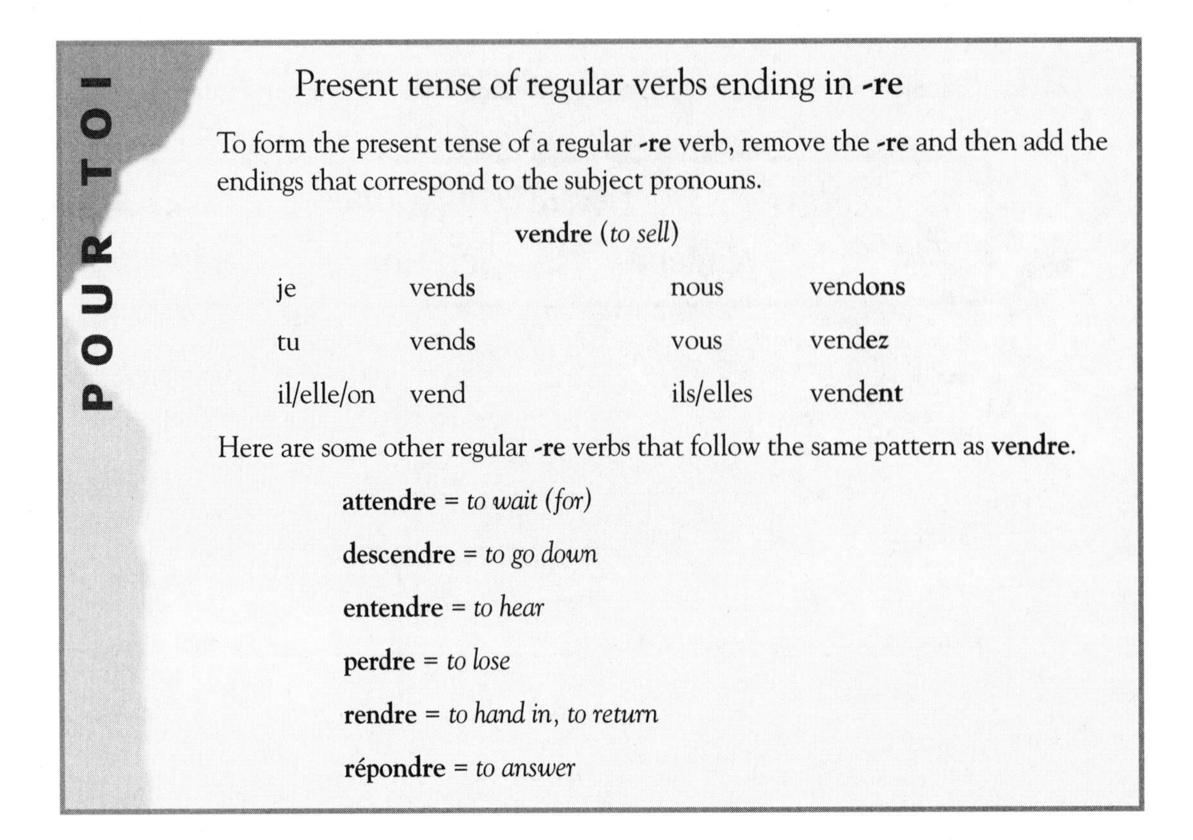

POUR TOI

Present tense of regular verbs ending in -re

To form the present tense of a regular **-re** verb, remove the **-re** and then add the endings that correspond to the subject pronouns.

vendre (*to sell*)

je	vend**s**	nous	vend**ons**
tu	vend**s**	vous	vend**ez**
il/elle/on	vend	ils/elles	vend**ent**

Here are some other regular **-re** verbs that follow the same pattern as **vendre**.

attendre = *to wait (for)*

descendre = *to go down*

entendre = *to hear*

perdre = *to lose*

rendre = *to hand in, to return*

répondre = *to answer*

22 To earn money for their upcoming trip to France, many students have part-time jobs. Say what they sell, using the verb **vendre**.

1. Assia travaille dans une boutique où elle ______________________ des pantalons, des pulls et des chemises.
2. Paul et son frère ______________________ des chaussures.
3. Vous ______________________ des dictionnaires et des livres dans un magasin.
4. Nous ______________________ des anoraks au centre commercial.
5. Édouard et Renée ______________________ des hamburgers et des frites au fast-food.
6. Tu ______________________ des jeans et des tee-shirts dans une boutique.
7. Jean-Christophe ______________________ des cassettes et des CDs.
8. Je ______________________ des vélos.

23

After the final boys' and girls' soccer games of the season, many of the team members' family and friends wait for them. Tell whom everyone is waiting for, using the verb **attendre**.

1. Les parents de Dikembe ____________________ leur fils.
2. Gilberte ____________________ son ami Salim.
3. M. et Mme Harras ____________________ leurs filles.
4. Nous ____________________ notre petit frère.
5. Tu ____________________ ton amie Céline.
6. Olivier ____________________ ses deux sœurs.
7. J'____________________ ma demi-sœur.
8. Vous ____________________ vos deux cousins.

24

To complete each sentence, choose the most logical verb from the list below and write its appropriate form. Use each verb only once.

	descendre	*perdre*	RÉPONDRE
attendre	entendre	rendre	vendre

1. Qui ____________________ au téléphone?
2. Maman, je ne vais pas bien. Je ne ____________________ pas pour manger.
3. J'____________________ le bus avec mes amis.
4. Les élèves ____________________ le professeur qui parle devant la classe.
5. Vous ____________________ vos devoirs au professeur.
6. Nous ____________________ le match deux à quatre.
7. Qu'est-ce qu'on ____________________ dans la boutique là-bas?

25 Complete each sentence of the crossword puzzle with the correct form of **parler, finir** or **vendre**.

Across

1. Le cours de français... à dix heures.
3. Les étudiants... français avec la prof.
5. Mon père ne... pas français.
6. Est-ce que tu... des blousons et des anoraks?
7. Nous... l'interro en classe.
8. Tu... français et anglais, n'est-ce pas?

Down

1. Les élèves... leurs devoirs.
2. Nous ne... pas de pizza ici, Monsieur.
3. Nous... anglais aussi.
4. Vous ne... pas vos devoirs de sciences?
6. Nadine et Éric... des cassettes et des CDs au magasin.
7. Est-ce que tu... les devoirs de maths?

Unité 8 On fait les courses.

Leçon A

1 Find and circle the names of 13 food items in French. Then list them below the grid, adding **un, une** or **des** before each one.

P	O	M	M	E	D	E	T	E	R	R	E	W	U	K
Q	R	Z	D	T	Q	C	R	E	V	E	T	T	E	F
K	A	L	E	T	P	Z	E	M	U	G	É	L	F	S
C	N	M	J	O	C	E	V	A	I	Z	K	W	B	S
Z	G	R	H	R	Q	R	T	Y	T	O	K	J	J	K
N	E	R	A	A	Y	B	O	I	F	N	S	Z	O	N
B	T	B	E	C	M	A	C	F	T	H	A	M	I	I
N	E	A	N	O	S	S	I	O	P	S	Y	P	O	H
Z	T	K	L	T	Q	I	R	C	T	A	P	Y	O	Q
N	O	N	G	I	P	M	A	H	C	I	N	O	E	E
C	M	B	I	U	V	W	H	A	N	O	N	G	I	O
A	A	B	M	R	S	D	H	C	W	J	E	H	E	S
U	T	R	M	F	X	A	L	I	T	R	I	Q	B	G
D	E	I	G	Q	I	D	U	B	P	B	L	D	X	Z

2 Write three simple menus in French. Each menu begins with a vegetable entrée (course before the main dish). The main course, fish and vegetables, comes next. A dessert ends each menu. (You may want to refer back to pages 76-78 in your textbook for suggestions.) What would be a reasonable price in euros for each of these menus?

La Carte

Menu à__________ euros

Entrée:

____

Plat:

____

Dessert:

____

La Carte

Menu à__________ euros

Entrée:

____

Plat:

____

Dessert:

____

LA CARTE

Menu à__________ euros

Entrée:

____

Plat:

____

Dessert:

____

POUR TOI

Present tense of the irregular verb **vouloir**

Do you remember the forms of the verb **vouloir** (*to want*)?

je	veux	nous	voulons
tu	veux	vous	voulez
il/elle/on	veut	ils/elles	veulent

3 It's another cold, rainy day. Many students and teachers are talking about what they want to do when they get home. Complete their sentences, using the verb **vouloir**.

1. Marie-Hélène ____________________________ finir son livre.
2. Les frères de Karl ____________________________ écouter le reggae.
3. Nous ____________________________ faire des crêpes.
4. Christophe ____________________________ faire ses devoirs.
5. Tu ____________________________ dormir.
6. Vous ____________________________ jouer aux jeux vidéo.
7. Mes professeurs ________________________________ sortir avec leurs familles.
8. Je ____________________________ regarder un bon film à la télé.

4 As he waits for the métro, Frédéric hears a number of short conversations. Complete each sentence with the appropriate form of the verb **vouloir**.

1. — Qu'est-ce que tu ____________________________ faire samedi?
   — Je ____________________________ aller au centre commercial.
2. — Où ____________________________-vous aller en vacances?
   — Nous ____________________________ voyager en Espagne et en Italie.
3. — Est-ce que tes amis __________________________ manger à la cantine ou au fast-food?
   — Ils ____________________________ manger à la cantine.
4. — Patrick? ____________________________-il jouer au foot ou au basket?
   — Il ____________________________ jouer au basket.

5. — En été ma sœur et moi, nous ________________________ étudier à Paris.
   — Dans quelle école est-ce que vous ________________________ étudier?
6. — Éric et sa femme ________________________ aller au cinéma dimanche.
   — À quel cinéma ________________________-ils aller?

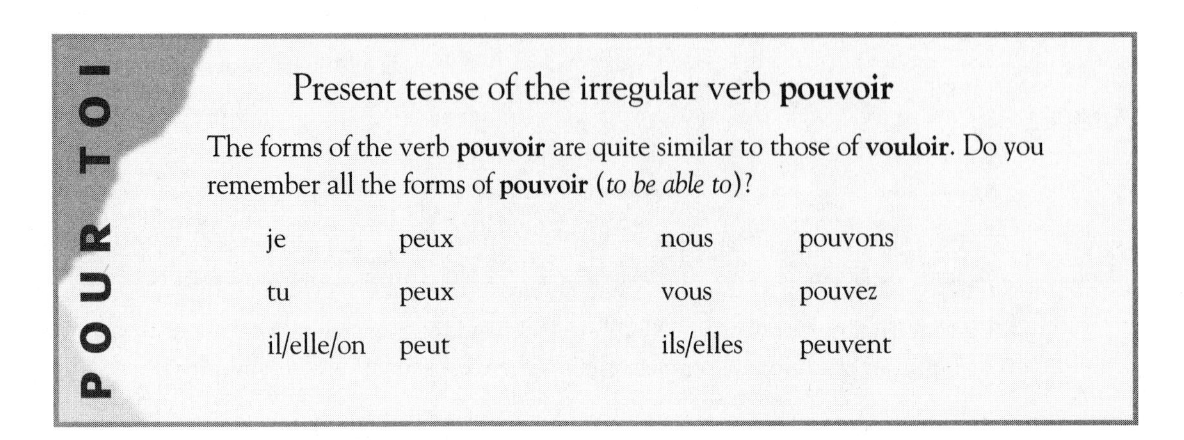

POUR TOI

Present tense of the irregular verb **pouvoir**

The forms of the verb **pouvoir** are quite similar to those of **vouloir**. Do you remember all the forms of **pouvoir** (*to be able to*)?

je	peux	nous	pouvons
tu	peux	vous	pouvez
il/elle/on	peut	ils/elles	peuvent

5 Lots of people are shopping at the Galeries Lafayette, a popular French department store. Suggest combinations of the illustrated items that the following people could buy without exceeding the amount of money that they have with them.

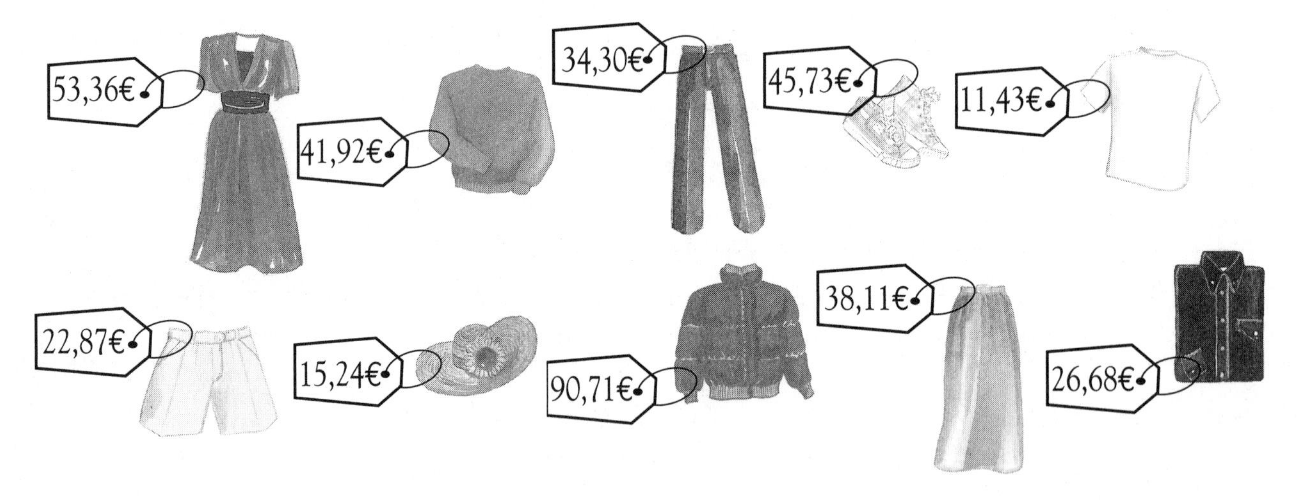

Modèle: Suzanne a soixante-seize euros vingt-deux.
Elle peut acheter la jupe, le tee-shirt et le chapeau.

1. Nicolas a soixante-seize euros vingt-deux.

   ____

2. Nous avons soixante euros quatre-vingt-dix-huit.

   ____

3. Vous avez cent vingt-neuf euros cinquante-huit.

4. Karine et Stéphanie ont quarante-cinq euros soixante-treize.

5. Tu as trente-huit euros onze.

6. J'ai quatre-vingt-quinze euros vingt-huit.

7. Raoul et son demi-frère ont soixante-huit euros soixante.

8. Mme Delon a cent trente-sept euros vingt.

6 Jean-Jacques, the new French exchange student, is curious about you and your friends. Answer his questions.

1. Est-ce que tes amis veulent manger à la cantine?

2. Est-ce que tu peux aller en boîte samedi soir?

3. Qu'est-ce que tu veux acheter au grand magasin?

4. Pourquoi est-ce que tu veux étudier le français?

5. Est-ce que nous pouvons étudier ensemble?

6. Est-ce que tu veux voyager en France un jour?

7. Est-ce que tu peux skier?

8. Est-ce que tu veux aller à l'université après l'école?

POUR TOI

Demonstrative adjectives

Demonstrative adjectives agree with the nouns they describe.

Singular			Plural
Masculine before a Consonant Sound	**Masculine before a Vowel Sound**	**Feminine**	
ce champignon	**cet** oignon	**cette** tomate	**ces** légumes

7 Accompanied by her French host mother, Suzy often goes to the open-air market. There she hears many short conversations between customers and vendors. Complete the sentences she hears with **ce**, **cet**, **cette** or **ces**.

1. — Bonjour, Monsieur! Vous désirez?

   — Je voudrais _______________ champignons.
2. — Et vous, Madame?

   — Combien coûte _______________ orange?
3. — Et alors? Vous, Monsieur et Madame?

   — Nous voulons _______________ fromage.
4. — Oui, Mademoiselle?

   — _______________ oignon, est-il frais?
5. — Bonjour, Madame! Vous désirez?

   — Je vais acheter _______________ crevettes, Monsieur.
6. — Vous voulez, Monsieur?

   — Je voudrais _______________ poissons pour ma bouillabaisse.
7. — Bonjour, Mme Clerc! Nous avons des quiches et des crêpes aujourd'hui.

   — Bonjour, Mme Loisel! _________________ grande quiche, combien coûte-t-elle?
8. — Et je voudrais un café, Madame.

   — Attention, Madame! _______________ café est très chaud.

8 Marie-Élise has three friends with birthdays next week. Since she has only a limited amount to spend on gifts, she goes to the **marché aux puces**. Hoping to stay within her budget, Marie-Élise asks for prices of various items. Complete her questions with **ce**, **cet**, **cette** or **ces**.

1. Combien coûtent ______________ vieux livres?
2. S'il vous plaît, ______________ robe jaune coûte combien?
3. Ah bon, et ______________ chapeau?
4. Oh là là! Est-ce que ______________ anorak gris est cher?
5. Et ______________ vieux calendrier?
6. J'aime beaucoup ______________ stylos. Ils coûtent combien?
7. ______________ vieille pendule, c'est combien?
8. Et ______________ dessin japonais?

9 Rearrange the following words to make logical sentences.

1. minérale/froide/eau/est/très/cette

   ____

2. fromage/veut/Michel/au/sandwich/ce

   ____

3. chocolat/cette/bonne/glace/est/au

   ____

4. oranges/ils/aujourd'hui/ces/manger/peuvent

   ____

5. va/ces/ma/sandwichs/belle-mère/acheter

   ____

6. ces/manger/terre/voudrais/de/je/pommes

   ____

7. faire/salade/Claire/cette/peut

   ____

8. ces/voulons/crevettes/nous/manger

   ____

Leçon B

10 Unscramble the letters in each food item. Then use the letters in the boxes and rearrange them to find the mystery word, the French expression for "Enjoy your meal!"

1. eeautbgt [ ] ___ ___ ___ ___ ___ ___ ___
2. aaeioynmns ___ ___ ___ [ ] ___ ___ ___ ___ ___ ___
3. nuicaosss ___ ___ ___ ___ ___ ___ ___ ___ [ ]
4. tial ___ [ ] ___ ___
5. otelup [ ] ___ ___ ___ ___ ___
6. crop [ ] ___ ___ ___
7. tâpé ___ ___ ___ [ ]
8. tyruoa ___ ___ ___ ___ ___ [ ]
9. eioruftcn ___ ___ ___ ___ [ ] ___ ___ ___ ___
10. atugeâ ___ ___ [ ] ___ ___ ___

In French, "Enjoy your meal!" is ______________________________

11 Alexandre's mother wants him to do some grocery shopping at various stores. List two items that she might ask him to buy at each place. (You may first want to review the vocabulary on page 266 of your textbook.)

Modèle: au supermarché
la moutarde, la mayonnaise

1. à la boucherie ______________________________
2. à la pâtisserie ______________________________
3. à la crémerie ______________________________
4. à la charcuterie ______________________________
5. à la boulangerie ______________________________

The partitive article

POUR TOI

To express "some" or "any," combine **de** with a singular definite article (**le**, **la** or **l'**). The plural combined form is **des**.

Mon petit frère mange **du** yaourt comme dessert.

Patrick veut **de la** moutarde avec son hot-dog.

De l'eau minérale, s'il vous plaît. J'ai soif.

Je voudrais **des** frites.

12 Kathy is planning a picnic for her host family in France before she returns to the United States. Put each item on her shopping list under the name of the store where she will buy it, indicating that she will buy "some" of each item (**du**, **de la**, **de l'**, **des**).

BAGUETTES tartes aux fraises yaourt moutarde
eau minérale mayonnaise coca
jambon beurre fromage pâté poulet

à la boucherie	à la boulangerie	à la charcuterie
______	______	______
______	______	______
______	______	______
______	______	______
______	______	______

à la crémerie	à la pâtisserie	au supermarché
______	______	______
______	______	______
______	______	______
______	______	______
______	______	______

13

Many students and teachers are eating in the school cafeteria today. Complete each of their sentences with the appropriate form of "some" or "any."

1. Nous voulons manger _______________ frites et _______________ poisson.
2. Je voudrais _______________ omelette et _______________ haricots verts.
3. Pauline et Marc veulent _______________ hot-dogs avec _______________ moutarde.
4. Le professeur d'histoire veut _______________ tarte aux fraises et _______________ café.
5. Carole veut _______________ fromage, _______________ pain et _______________ eau minérale.
6. M. Atienzo veut _______________ poulet et _______________ petits pois.
7. Comme dessert Mme Adoux veut _______________ gâteau et _______________ glace.
8. Sandrine et son amie veulent _______________ pâté et _______________ pain.

14

As they return home from school or work, everyone in the Perrier family is hungry or thirsty. Complete what they say with **du, de la, de l', des** or **le, la, l', les**.

1. — Maman, il y a _______________ soupe? Il fait froid aujourd'hui!
2. — Non, ce soir nous avons _______________ poulet et _______________ pommes de terre.
3. — Ah bon, et _______________ salade aussi?
4. — Je voudrais _______________ légumes.
5. — Moi aussi, j'aime _______________ légumes. Tu préfères _______________ haricots verts ou _______________ champignons?
6. — Maman, je peux avoir _______________ pain et _______________ confiture?
7. — Mais oui. Et tu veux aussi _______________ eau minérale?
8. — Qu'est-ce qu'il y a comme dessert? _______________ yaourt ou _______________ glace?
9. — _______________ glace au chocolat.
10. — Super! J'adore _______________ glace au chocolat.

The partitive article in negative sentences

POUR TOI

Remember that **du, de la, de l'** and **des** change to **de** or **d'** in negative sentences.

Christian mange **du** poisson.	Son frère ne mange pas **de** poisson.
Tu veux **de l'**eau minérale?	Non, je ne veux pas **d'**eau minérale.

15 It's a hot summer evening. Everyone at the café is thirsty, not hungry. How do they answer the server's questions?

Modèles: Vous voulez un sandwich au fromage?
Non, je ne veux pas de sandwich au fromage. J'ai soif.

Vous voulez de l'eau minérale?
Oui, je veux bien. J'ai soif.

1. Vous voulez un dessert?

 ____

2. Vous voulez un jus d'orange?

 ____

3. Vous voulez un steak-frites?

 ____

4. Vous voulez des crêpes?

 ____

5. Vous voulez une limonade?

 ____

6. Vous voulez une quiche?

 ____

7. Vous voulez un coca?

 ____

8. Vous voulez de la glace?

 ____

16 Khaled is lactose intolerant, so he declines anything made with milk products. What does he say when offered the following foods and beverages?

Modèles: Du lait?
Non, je ne veux pas de lait.

De l'eau minérale?
Oui, je veux de l'eau minérale.

1. Du coca? ______
2. Des croissants? ______
3. De l'omelette? ______
4. Du fromage? ______
5. Du yaourt? ______
6. Du camembert? ______
7. De la glace? ______
8. Des pommes? ______

POUR TOI

Expressions of quantity

Expressions of quantity are followed by **de** or **d'** and a noun.

assez de	*enough*
beaucoup de	*a lot of, many*
combien de	*how much, how many*
(un) peu de	*(a) little, few*
trop de	*too much, too many*
un morceau de	*a piece of*
une tranche de	*a slice of*
un pot de	*a jar of*
une boîte de	*a can of*
une bouteille de	*a bottle of*
un kilo de	*a kilogram of*

Combien **de** jambon voulez-vous?

Je voudrais trois tranches **de** jambon.

17 Complete the crossword puzzle with the most appropriate expression of quantity.

Across

1. Nous avons... de tomates.
3. Élise achète un... de raisins.
6. Est-ce que tu as une... de petits pois?
8. Voulez-vous un... de fromage?
9. Avez-vous un... de moutarde?
10. Non, merci. J'ai... de ketchup pour mon hamburger.

Down

1. Alain a une... d'eau minérale.
2. ... de lait achetez-vous?
4. As-tu un... de pain?
5. Je voudrais une... de jambon pour mon sandwich.
7. Tu veux du dessert? Nous avons... de gâteau.

18 Paul works at a small grocery store in St.-Gilles-Croix-de-Vie. When customers request certain items, he frequently needs to ask them how much of each item they want. How does he respond to their requests?

Modèle: Des pommes, s'il vous plaît.
Combien de pommes voulez-vous?

1. Des oranges, s'il vous plaît.

____

2. Des carottes, s'il vous plaît.

____

3. Des œufs, s'il vous plaît.

____

4. Des tomates, s'il vous plaît.

____

5. Des pommes de terre, s'il vous plaît.

____

6. Des oignons, s'il vous plaît.

____

7. Des crevettes, s'il vous plaît.

____

8. Des champignons, s'il vous plaît.

____

19 Part of Paul's job at the grocery store is to complete certain orders. Help him do this by choosing from the list the most appropriate expression of quantity for each item.

un morceau de	une tranche de	un kilo de
une bouteille de	une boîte de	un pot de

Modèle: *un kilo de* pommes

1. _______________ jambon
2. _______________ fromage
3. _______________ confiture
4. _______________ haricots verts
5. _______________ eau minérale
6. _______________ coca
7. _______________ moutarde
8. _______________ pâté
9. _______________ lait
10. _______________ petits pois

Leçon C

20 Find and circle the names of ten fruits in French.

21 Sandra's little sister doesn't remember the names of many fruits in French, but she is able to describe them. What is she describing?

1. Un fruit rouge, vert ou jaune est.... ______________________
2. Deux petits fruits rouges pour faire les tartes sont....______________________
3. Un fruit long et jaune est.... ______________________
4. Un fruit vert et long est.... ______________________
5. Un fruit qui est jaune à l'extérieur et blanc à l'intérieur est.... ______________________

6. Un très petit fruit vert ou noir est.... ____________________
7. Un fruit orange qui vient de Floride est.... ____________________
8. Trois fruits qui sont orange à l'intérieur sont.... ____________________

POUR TOI

Comparative of adjectives

Do you remember how to compare people and things in French?

plus (*more*)	+	adjective	+	**que** (*than*)
moins (*less*)	+	adjective	+	**que** (*than*)
aussi (*as*)	+	adjective	+	**que** (*as*)

Les fraises sont **plus chères que** les pommes.

22 Gilberte works at a small grocery store on the weekends. As she stocks the fruits that have just arrived, she compares their relative sizes. Record her comparisons, using a form of the adjective **petit**.

Modèle: fraises/melons
Les fraises sont plus petites que les melons.

1. raisins/pommes
____
2. pêches/fraises
____
3. oranges/pommes
____
4. pastèques/bananes
____
5. poires/cerises
____
6. fraises/pêches
____

7. cerises/raisins

____

8. melons/pastèques

____

23 Imagine that you're shopping for clothes in France. As the salesclerk tells you prices of the items you're considering, make a note to yourself comparing these prices.

Modèle: Les pulls jaunes coûtent 15,24 euros, et les pulls rouges coûtent 18,29 euros.
Les pulls jaunes sont moins chers que les pulls rouges.

1. La robe bleue coûte 44,97 euros, et la robe blanche coûte 33,54 euros.

____

2. Les jeans coûtent 76,22 euros, et les pantalons coûtent 37,35 euros.

____

3. L'anorak coûte 132,63 euros, et le blouson coûte 132,63 euros.

____

4. Le short vert coûte 19,06 euros, et le short orange coûte 12,96 euros.

____

5. Les chaussures coûtent 65,55 euros, et les baskets coûtent 83,85 euros.

____

6. Le costume coûte 205,81 euros, et le tailleur coûte 205,81 euros.

____

7. La jupe beige coûte 32,78 euros, et la jupe courte coûte 26,68 euros.

____

8. Le tee-shirt coûte 14,48 euros, et le sweat coûte 24,39 euros.

____

24 How would you compare the following people, places and things?

Modèle: l'été/l'hiver (beau)
L'été est plus beau que l'hiver.

1. la France/les États-Unis (grand)

 ____

2. les filles/les garçons (bavard)

 ____

3. les vêtements français/les vêtements américains (joli)

 ____

4. ma mère/mon père (généreux)

 ____

5. un anorak/un manteau (long)

 ____

6. une télévision/un ordinateur (cher)

 ____

7. les chats/les chiens (intelligent)

 ____

8. la Martinique/la Guadeloupe (français)

 ____

Unité 9 À la maison

Leçon A

1 Unscramble the letters to spell the names of household furnishings.

1. tuuaielf ____________________
2. rimaoer ____________________
3. riveé ____________________
4. ilt ____________________
5. paénac ____________________
6. eginobari ____________________
7. satip ____________________
8. lapadrc ____________________
9. nuceièisir ____________________
10. hoduce ____________________

2 Draw a simple floor plan of your house or apartment like the one on page 296 of your textbook. Label the rooms and pieces of furniture in French.

3 Complete the crossword puzzle with the French expressions for the rooms in a house and household furnishings.

Across

6. On trouve le lait dans le....
7. Dans une chambre on peut trouver des vêtements dans une....
10. Mon appartement a quatre...: un salon, une cuisine, une salle à manger et une chambre.
11. On utilise souvent la... pour faire chauffer (*heat*) la soupe.
12. On mange souvent dans la... à manger.
14. Un... peut remplacer un salon.
15. On a souvent des... de la famille dans le salon.

Down

1. On trouve beaucoup d'... dans un immeuble.
2. On trouve un lit dans une....
3. On trouve souvent les livres et une lampe sur un....
4. Les W.-C. sont aussi les....
5. On trouve une... dans la salle de bains.
6. On prépare les gâteaux dans le....
8. On trouve souvent une table ou un bureau avec une....
9. On a souvent un canapé et un... dans le salon.
13. Dans une chambre il y a toujours un....

4 Based on the drawing you made in Activity 2, write six sentences about your house or apartment. Describe its rooms and the pieces of furniture in each one.

Modèle: *Dans notre salon il y a un canapé et deux fauteuils.*
Dans ma chambre il y a une stéréo et....

____

____

____

____

____

____

____

____

5 Read the description of the rooms and furniture in Sandra's house. Then, next to the illustrations of various household furnishings, tell how many of each item there are in her house.

Dans notre salon il y a deux canapés et deux fauteuils. Il y a aussi deux petites tables et un bureau. Sur une de ces tables il y a une lampe et une photo de la famille. Dans notre séjour nous avons un grand canapé et trois fauteuils. Dans la chambre de mes parents il y a un grand lit et un petit fauteuil avec un bureau. Ils ont aussi une armoire dans leur chambre. Dans ma chambre il y a un grand lit, un bureau, une chaise et une stéréo. Sur mon bureau il y a une lampe. Nous avons deux salles de bains. Dans ma salle de bains il y a une douche, et dans la salle de bains de mes parents il y a une douche et une baignoire.

Modèle:

deux

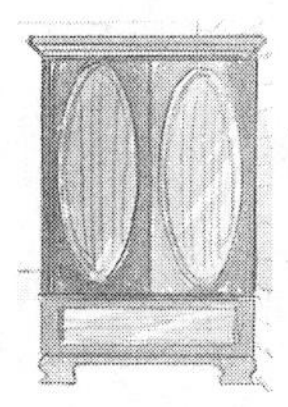

1. ____________________

2. ____________________

3. ________________ 4. ________________

5. ________________ 6. ________________

7. ________________ 8. ________________

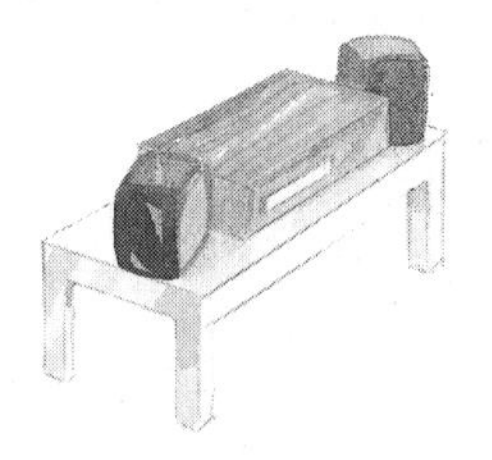

9. ________________ 10. ________________

De + plural adjectives

POUR TOI

Des changes to **de** before a plural adjective that precedes a noun.

Tu as **de** nouvelles lampes?

Use **des** before a noun that precedes a plural adjective.

Tu as **des** lampes italiennes?

---

6 A new department store has just opened in your neighborhood. Complete the store's newspaper ad with **des** or **de**.

1. Pour les enfants il y a _______________ petites chemises et _______________ petits pantalons.
2. Pour les femmes d'affaires il y a _______________ tailleurs beiges ou noirs avec _______________ chemises roses ou violettes.
3. Pour les hommes il y a _______________ costumes marron et noirs et _______________ jolies chemises beiges ou grises.
4. Pour les filles qui aiment les sports il y a _______________ petits tee-shirts et _______________ shorts blancs.
5. Pour les garçons qui jouent au basket il y a _______________ baskets blanches ou noires.
6. Pour les filles il y a _______________ belles jupes bleues ou rouges avec _______________ chemises blanches ou avec _______________ petits pulls.
7. Pour les garçons on peut trouver _______________ blousons bleus, blancs ou rouges.
8. Pour sortir, les femmes peuvent trouver _______________ très belles robes longues.

7 Mme Lamoureux is planning a large family celebration. She calls various grocers to order exactly what she wants. Complete her short conversations with **des** or **de**.

1. — Bonjour, Monsieur. Avez-vous _______________ fraises fraîches aujourd'hui?

   — Mais oui, Madame. Combien _______________ kilos de fraises voulez-vous?

2. — M. Feria? Je cherche _______________ pastèques... pour 20 personnes.

   — Bon, Madame. J'ai _______________ belles pastèques de deux à quatre kilos.

3. — Bonjour. C'est Mme Sachs? Bon, je voudrais acheter _______________ haricots verts.

   — Ah, Mme Lamoureux. Combien _______________ kilos de haricots verts voulez-vous?

4. — C'est le supermarché STOC? Avez-vous _______________ crevettes aujourd'hui?

   — Oui, Madame. Nous avons beaucoup _______________ jolies crevettes.

5. — M. Torti? C'est Mme Lamoureux. Je voudrais _______________ petits pois très frais... pour 20 personnes.

   — Oui, Madame. _______________ petits pois frais pour quel jour?

6. — Bonjour, Mademoiselle. C'est la charcuterie Bérain? Avez-vous _______________ tranches de jambon aujourd'hui?

   — Ah oui, Madame. Nous avons _______________ très bonnes tranches de jambon.

Leçon B

8

Write the letter of the matching English equivalent of each French expression.

_____ 1.	une fleur	A. tree
_____ 2.	le sous-sol	B. garden, lawn
_____ 3.	le grenier	C. ground floor
_____ 4.	le garage	D. floor above the ground floor
_____ 5.	une maison	E. stairs, staircase
_____ 6.	un arbre	F. flower
_____ 7.	le premier étage	G. house
_____ 8.	l'entrée	H. basement
_____ 9.	la voiture	I. garage
_____ 10.	le rez-de-chaussée	J. entrance
_____ 11.	l'escalier	K. attic
_____ 12.	le jardin	L. car

9

Think of your favorite two-story house. You might choose one in your neighborhood, one that you've seen in a movie or one in a magazine. Then name the rooms on each level and describe what's in each room.

Modèle: Au premier étage
Il y a une grande chambre avec un lit, un fauteuil, une télé....

Au rez-de-chaussée

____

____

____

____

____

____

____

____

Au premier étage

____

____

____

____

____

____

____

____

10 Complete Élisabeth's description of her grandparents' home in Normandy. Use each of the listed words only once.

voiture	cuisine	SALON	chambre	premier étage
FLEURS	sous-sol	garage	rez-de-chaussée	arbres

La maison de mes grands-parents est assez petite. Il y a deux étages, le ______________ et le premier étage. Il n'y a pas de ______________. Quand vous entrez dans leur maison, le ______________ est à gauche (*on the left*). Dans cette pièce il y a une piano, un canapé et des fauteuils. À droite (*on the right*) on trouve la ______________ avec le frigo et le four. Pour aller dans la ______________ de mes grands-parents, il est nécessaire de monter (*go up*) au ______________. Ils ont une belle chambre avec un grand lit. Il y a toujours beaucoup de ______________ du jardin dans leur chambre. Dans leur jardin il y a aussi beaucoup d'______________. Mes grands-parents prennent souvent l'autobus parce qu'ils n'ont pas de ______________. Donc, ils n'ont pas de ______________.

Present tense of the irregular verb **prendre**

Do you remember the forms of the verb **prendre** (*to take*)?

je	prends	nous	prenons
tu	prends	vous	prenez
il/elle/on	prend	ils/elles	prennent

POUR TOI

11 Everyone is talking about what they plan to take along with them on the annual **École de Neige** (*Ski School*) trip. Complete their short conversations with the appropriate form of the verb **prendre**.

1. — Tu ________________ tes vieilles bottes de ski?

   — Non, je ________________ les bottes de ski de ma sœur.

2. — Isabelle et Éric? Est-ce que vous ________________ vos nouveaux anoraks?

   — Oui, et nous ________________ nos pulls et nos jeans aussi.

3. — Chloé et Magali ________________ beaucoup de chaussettes. Et toi?

   — Moi? Je ________________ beaucoup de pulls.

4. — Gilberte et toi, vous ________________ vos skis?

   — Oui, nous ________________ nos skis et nos bâtons (*ski poles*).

5. — Patrick et Raphaël ________________ des jeans.

   — Oui, mais ils ne ________________ pas de pantalons.

6. — Fabrice ________________ un magazine de ski.

   — Et moi, je ________________ mes CDs.

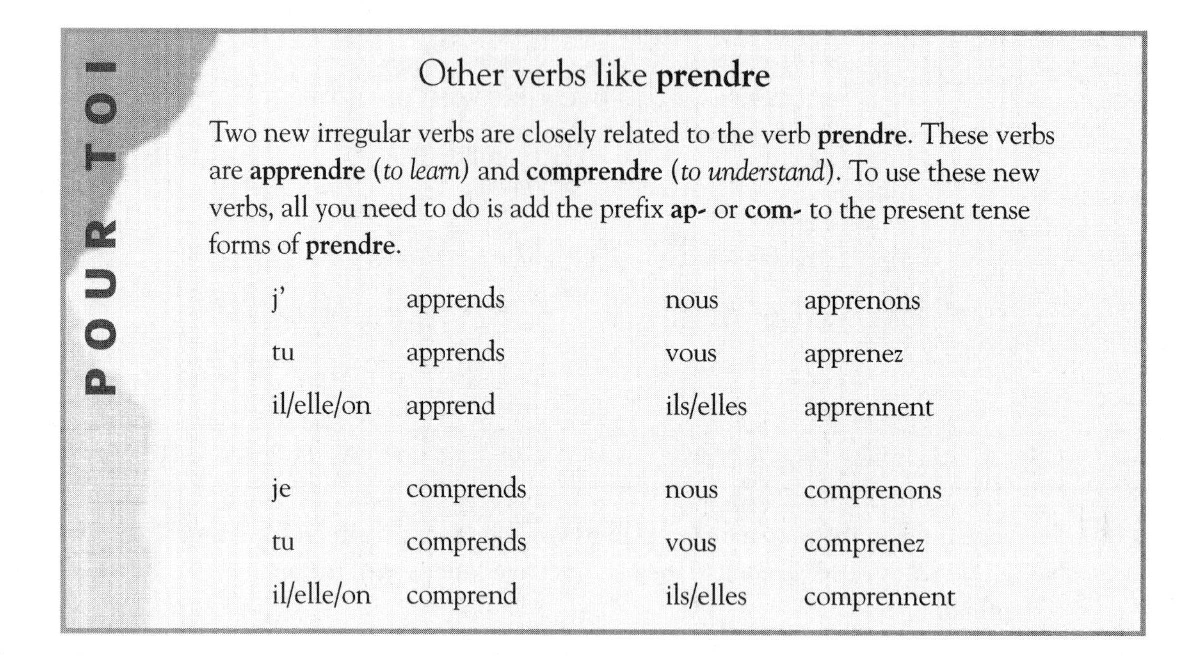

POUR TOI

Other verbs like **prendre**

Two new irregular verbs are closely related to the verb **prendre**. These verbs are **apprendre** (*to learn*) and **comprendre** (*to understand*). To use these new verbs, all you need to do is add the prefix **ap-** or **com-** to the present tense forms of **prendre**.

j'	apprends	nous	apprenons
tu	apprends	vous	apprenez
il/elle/on	apprend	ils/elles	apprennent

je	comprends	nous	comprenons
tu	comprends	vous	comprenez
il/elle/on	comprend	ils/elles	comprennent

12 At the local **Maison des Jeunes et de la Culture** (*youth center*), there are always lots of activities to interest teenagers in the neighborhood. Malick is telling what his friends are learning how to do. Complete his sentences with the appropriate form of the verb **apprendre**.

1. Le petit frère d'Ahmed ____________________ à jouer au basket.
2. Chantal et ses deux amies anglaises ____________________ à préparer des desserts français.
3. Hervé, Salim et moi, nous ____________________ à jouer au foot.
4. Tu ____________________ à faire du roller.
5. Vous ____________________ à jouer au tennis.
6. Benjamin et Ousmane ____________________ à jouer de la guitare.
7. Moi, j'____________________ à faire de la poterie.
8. Yasmine ____________________ à jouer au volley.

Names of languages

POUR TOI

Do you know the names of these languages in French?

le français	*French*	**l'italien**	*Italian*
l'anglais	*English*	**le japonais**	*Japanese*
l'allemand	*German*	**le russe**	*Russian*
l'espagnol	*Spanish*	**le suédois**	*Swedish*
le chinois	*Chinese*	**le portugais**	*Portuguese*

13 The first meeting of your school's Foreign Students' Club is very quiet. Only a few people are talking because most students don't understand the languages spoken by the new members. Tell which languages the following people don't understand, using the appropriate forms of the verb **comprendre**.

Modèle: Joe ne parle pas avec Lucila qui vient d'Espagne.
Joe ne comprend pas l'espagnol.

1. Nous ne parlons pas avec Dieter qui vient d'Allemagne.

 ____

2. Pete ne parle pas avec Li qui vient de Chine.

 ____

3. Ben et son demi-frère ne parlent pas avec Boris qui vient de Russie.

 ____

4. Les filles du professeur de maths ne parlent pas avec Maria qui vient d'Italie.

 ____

5. Vous ne parlez pas avec Bengt qui vient de Suède.

 ____

6. Je ne parle pas avec Michiko qui vient du Japon.

 ____

7. Tu ne parles pas avec Paolo qui vient du Portugal.

 ____

8. Terry ne parle pas avec Laure qui vient de France.

 ____

14 The Radio France choir members are discussing their upcoming trip to Europe. Complete each sentence of their short conversations with the appropriate form of the verb **prendre**, **apprendre** or **comprendre**.

1. — Mathilde, est-ce que tu ________________________ à parler italien?

   — Non, j'________________________ à parler espagnol.

2. — Le professeur de musique ne ________________________ pas l'allemand.

   — C'est vrai, mais il ________________________ l'italien.

3. — Est-ce que Charles et Djamel ________________________ leurs dictionnaires d'espagnol?

   — Oui, et leur sœur ________________________ son dictionnaire d'allemand.

4. — Ma mère vient aussi, et elle ________________________ à parler italien.

   — C'est bon! Ma mère et mon père ________________________ seulement (*only*) le français.

5. — Les parents de Valérie viennent, et ils ________________________ des cassettes en espagnol.

   — Magnifique! Moi, je ________________________ mes cassettes en anglais.

POUR TOI

The imperative

To give commands and make suggestions, use the **tu**, **vous** and **nous** forms of the verb without the subjects. Note that the **tu** form of an **-er** verb drops the **s**.

Tu vas au cinéma.	**Va** au cinéma!
Vous finissez vos devoirs.	**Finissez** vos devoirs!
Nous prenons des sandwichs.	**Prenons** des sandwichs!

To form a negative command, put **ne** before the verb and **pas** after it.

N'achetez **pas** ce CD!

15 Frédéric is babysitting his younger sister. Write what he tells her to do or not to do.

Modèles: manger une orange
Mange une orange!

manger beaucoup de chocolat
Ne mange pas beaucoup de chocolat!

1. manger une salade

____

2. prendre de l'eau

____

3. faire du roller dans la maison

____

4. téléphoner en Allemagne

____

5. jouer avec le chien

____

6. aller dans ta chambre

____

7. finir tes devoirs

____

8. étudier pour l'interro

____

16 Mme Grincheux is the substitute teacher in French class today. Write what she tells the students to do or not to do.

Modèles: parler français en classe
Parlez français en classe!

parler anglais en classe
Ne parlez pas anglais en classe!

1. écouter les cassettes en français

 ____

2. écouter le rock

 ____

3. parler avec vos amis

 ____

4. manger en classe

 ____

5. prendre vos cahiers

 ____

6. donner vos interros aux autres élèves

 ____

7. finir vos devoirs pour demain

 ____

8. faire les devoirs de maths

 ____

17 Imagine that you meet some French exchange students at a party. Suggest what you can all do together.

Modèle: manger des chips
Mangeons des chips!

1. parler français

 ____

2. écouter la techno

 ____

3. danser

 ____

4. regarder une vidéocassette en français

 ____

5. prendre des apéros

 ____

6. manger de la pizza

 ____

7. jouer au foot demain

 ____

8. aller au concert ensemble

 ____

Leçon C

18 Find and circle the names of 12 items in a French table setting.

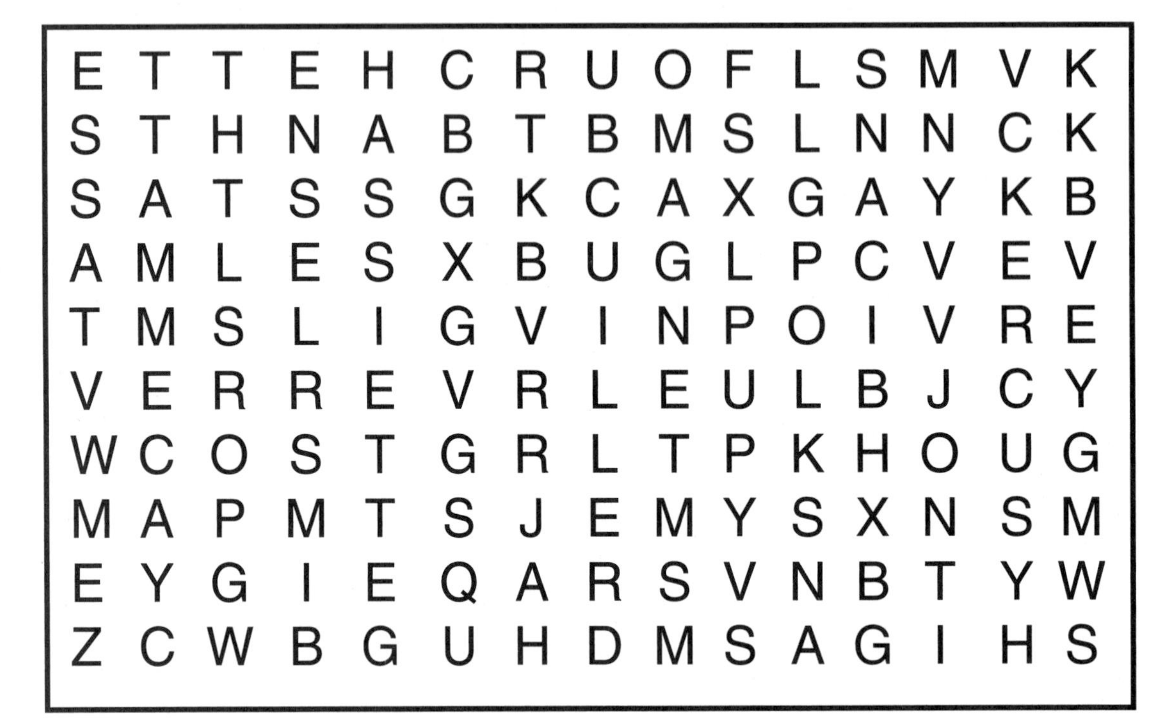

19 Draw a typical table setting for a special dinner. Then label each item on the table in French. Make your drawing large enough so that you can add and label some typical foods that would be on the table, such as bread and butter.

20 Based on the drawing you made in Activity 19, write a description of your table setting. Tell the location of at least six items.

Modèle: *La serviette est à gauche de la fourchette.*

____

____

____

____

____

____

____

____

21 Tell what you typically eat for breakfast, lunch and dinner. Use as much of the French food vocabulary that you have learned as possible. Also tell at what time you eat each meal.

1. Je prends le petit déjeuner à ____________________.

   Au petit déjeuner je prends ______________________________

   ____

   ____

   ____.

2. Je prends le déjeuner à ____________________.

   Au déjeuner je prends ______________________________

   ____

   ____

   ____.

3. Je prends le dîner à ____________________.

   Au dîner je prends ______________________________

   ____

   ____

   ____.

POUR TOI

Present tense of the irregular verb **mettre**

Do you remember the forms of the verb **mettre** (*to put, to put on, to set*)?

je	mets	nous	mettons
tu	mets	vous	mettez
il/elle/on	met	ils/elles	mettent

22 Nadia is telling what everyone in the family is putting on the table to prepare for her grandmother's birthday dinner. Complete her sentences with the appropriate forms of the verb **mettre**.

1. Mes parents ____________________ la nappe et les serviettes.
2. Danièle et moi, nous ____________________ les assiettes.
3. Vous ____________________ les verres et les tasses.
4. Béatrice et sa petite sœur ____________________ les bols.
5. Tu ____________________ le sel, le poivre et le sucre.
6. Ma tante Adèle ____________________ les fourchettes et les couteaux.
7. Et moi, je ____________________ les cuillers.

23 The Senghor family is moving to a new apartment in Paris and their neighbors are helping them. Mme Senghor tells where everyone is putting the family's things. Write what she says, adding the appropriate forms of the verb **mettre**.

Modèle: tu/la lampe/sur la table
Tu mets la lampe sur la table.

1. Papa et moi, nous/le tapis dans le salon

____

2. Amine et toi, vous/le canapé dans le séjour

____

3. Karim et son frère/le grand lit dans notre chambre

____

4. tu/ton bureau dans ta chambre

____

5. Nora et sa sœur/les assiettes dans le placard

____

6. Latifa/la stéréo dans le séjour

____

7. je/mes robes dans l'armoire

____

---

24 Thérèse describes what she and her family are going to do. Complete her sentences to say what they are putting on in order to be appropriately dressed. Use each choice in the list only once.

un maillot de bain	**une chemise et un pantalon**
un tee-shirt, un short et des baskets	**une robe**
une chemise et un costume	**un tee-shirt, un short et des tennis**
un sweat et un jean	**des bottes, un anorak et un pantalon**

Modèle: Je vais jouer au basket.
Je *mets un tee-shirt, un short et des baskets*.

1. Ma sœur et toi, vous allez skier.
   Vous ____.
2. Mes frères vont jouer au tennis.
   Ils ____.
3. Nous allons travailler dans le jardin.
   Nous ____.
4. Mon grand-père va à la cathédrale.
   Il ____.
5. Ma grand-mère va faire les courses.
   Elle ____.
6. Tu vas nager.
   Tu ____.
7. Je vais au restaurant avec une amie.
   Je ____.

POUR TOI

Other verbs like **mettre**

Two new irregular verbs are closely related to the verb **mettre**. These verbs are **permettre** (*to permit, to allow*) and **promettre** (*to promise*). To use these new verbs, all you need to do is add the prefix **per-** or **pro-** to the present tense forms of **mettre**.

je	permets	nous	permettons
tu	permets	vous	permettez
il/elle/on	permet	ils/elles	permettent

je	promets	nous	promettons
tu	promets	vous	promettez
il/elle/on	promet	ils/elles	promettent

25 Mike's Belgian pen pal asked him questions about his school day in the United States. Complete each sentence of Mike's response with the appropriate form of **mettre**, **permettre** or **promettre**.

1. À la maison le matin, je ________________________ mes livres dans mon sac à dos.
2. Je ________________________ à ma mère de retourner à la maison après les cours, mais très souvent je fais du sport avec mes amis.
3. En cours de français le professeur ne ________________________ pas aux élèves de parler anglais.
4. Donc nous ________________________ au professeur de parler français.
5. Les professeurs ________________________ les devoirs pour demain au tableau.
6. Nous ________________________ à nos professeurs de faire nos devoirs.
7. Les professeurs ________________________ aux élèves de commencer leurs devoirs en classe.
8. Les professeurs ________________________ aux élèves de donner très peu de devoirs le weekend.

Unité 10 La santé

Leçon A

1 Find and circle the names of 10 parts of the body in French.

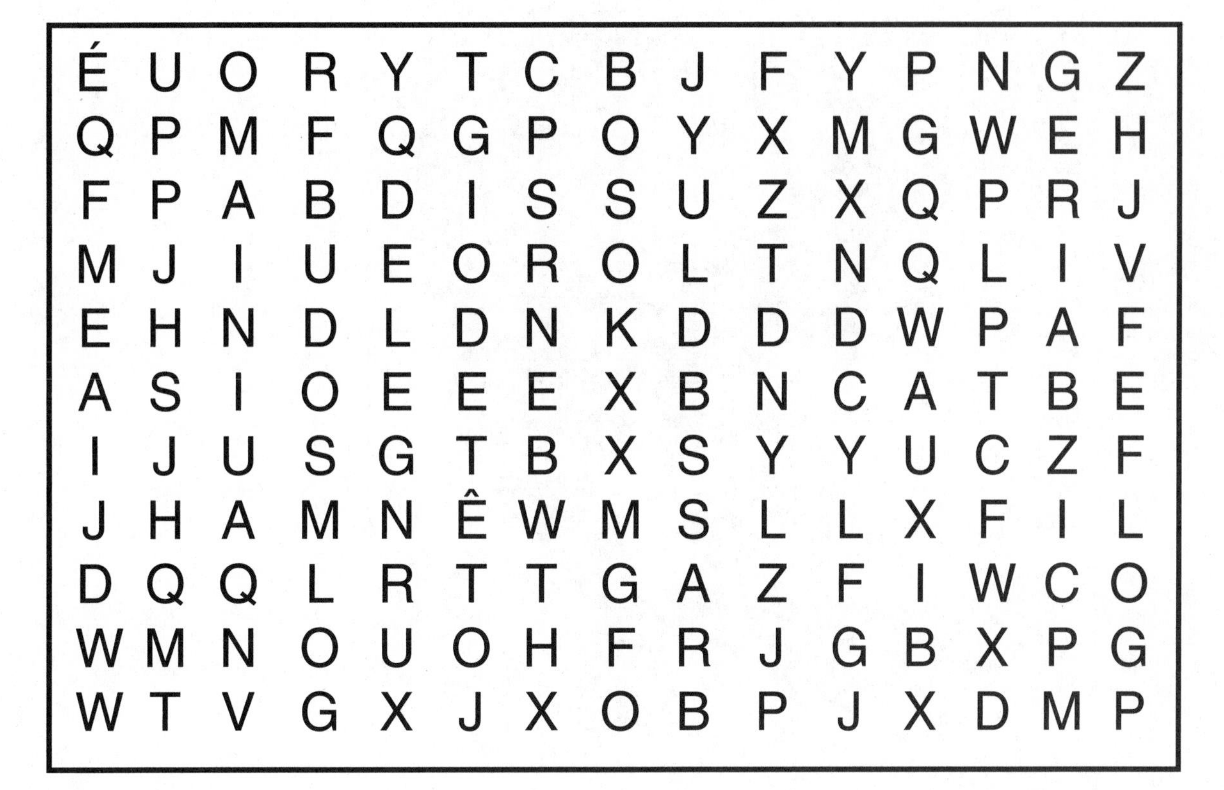

2 Label each of the indicated body parts, beginning with **le**, **la** or **l'**.

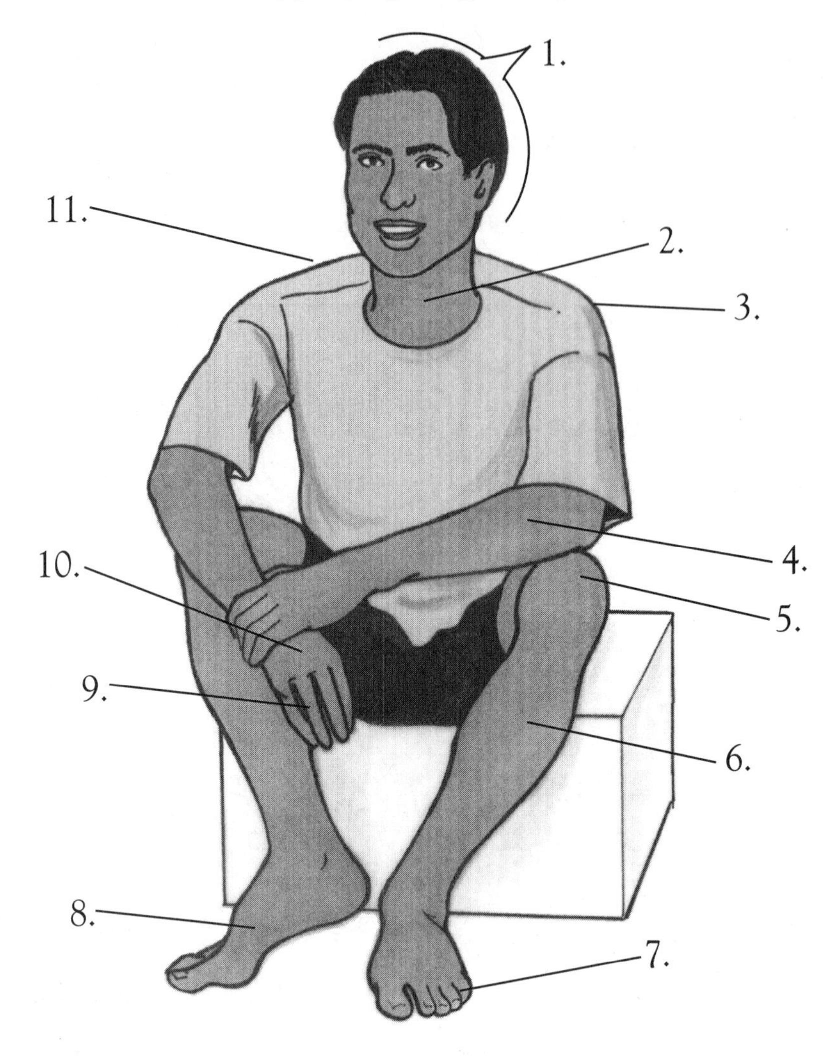

1. ______________________________
2. ______________________________
3. ______________________________
4. ______________________________
5. ______________________________
6. ______________________________
7. ______________________________
8. ______________________________
9. ______________________________
10. ______________________________
11. ______________________________

POUR TOI

Expressions with avoir

Forms of **avoir** are used in some French expressions where the verb "to be" is used in English. First of all, do you remember the forms of **avoir**?

j'	ai	nous	avons
tu	as	vous	avez
il/elle/on	a	ils/elles	ont

Certain expressions with **avoir** describe how we feel. Some of these expressions include:

avoir faim = *to be hungry*

avoir soif = *to be thirsty*

avoir froid = *to be cold*

avoir chaud = *to be warm, hot*

avoir peur (de) = *to be afraid (of)*

Tu **as peur**? *Are you afraid?*

Non, **j'ai froid**! *No, I'm cold!*

3 In each situation that follows, are the people warm, cold or afraid? Write your decision, completing the sentence with the appropriate form of **avoir chaud**, **avoir froid** or **avoir peur**.

Modèle: Maman voit (*sees*) un rat dans le grenier.
Elle *a peur*.

1. C'est l'été. Nous nageons dans l'océan.

   Nous ______________________________.

2. Mme Verchère et sa mère mettent leurs manteaux.

   Elles ______________________________.

3. Guillaume porte un short et un tee-shirt. Il fait du footing.

   Il ______________________________.

4. Tu portes un anorak et des bottes. Tu skies.

   Tu ______________________________.

5. Oh là là! Les agents de police viennent chez moi.

   J'____.

6. C'est l'hiver. Je voudrais un chocolat chaud.

   J'____.

7. La petite sœur de Claude voit un chien féroce.

   Elle ____.

8. Il fait du soleil. Vous mettez un maillot de bain.

   Vous ____.

4

Write the letter of the most appropriate response to each question or statement.

_____ 1.	Prenez-vous des omelettes?	A.	Tu as peur?
_____ 2.	Je voudrais un steak-frites.	B.	Vous avez chaud?
_____ 3.	C'est ton premier voyage transatlantique?	C.	Oui, j'ai froid.
_____ 4.	Attention! Il y a un serpent dans le jardin!	D.	Oui, et j'ai peur.
_____ 5.	Jeanne va mettre un short et un tee-shirt.	E.	Oui, nous avons faim.
_____ 6.	Nous allons nager dans le lac.	F.	Elle a chaud.
_____ 7.	Vous voulez un pull?	G.	Alors, vous avez soif.
_____ 8.	Je prends une limonade et Émilie prend un coca.	H.	Ah, tu as faim!

5

Karine plans to participate in the **Marathon de Paris** this spring. Her family doctor has suggested how she should prepare for the race. Write out his advice, beginning each sentence with **Il faut** or **Il ne faut pas**, as appropriate.

Modèles: faire du vélo
Il faut faire du vélo.

manger beaucoup de desserts
Il ne faut pas manger beaucoup de desserts.

1. manger beaucoup de fruits

   ____

2. prendre de l'alcool

   ____

3. manger beaucoup de chips

____

4. prendre de l'eau avec les repas

____

5. regarder la télé dix heures par jour

____

6. mettre des vêtements confortables

____

7. porter de bons tennis

____

8. dormir huit heures par jour

____

6 Laurence and her sister are planning a weekend visit to see their elderly grandparents. The girls' mother tells them what to do and what not to do during their stay. Write out her instructions, beginning each sentence with **Il faut** or **Il ne faut pas**.

Modèles: Faites le dîner samedi soir!
Il faut faire le dîner samedi soir.

Ne téléphone pas à vos amis!
Il ne faut pas téléphoner à vos amis.

1. Prenez assez d'euros pour le weekend!

____

2. N'arrivez pas après 20h00 vendredi soir!

____

3. Allez au supermarché samedi matin!

____

4. Préparez un bon déjeuner samedi!

____

5. Mettez la table!

____

6. Regardez le match de foot à la télé avec votre grand-père!

____

7. N'écoutez pas le rock!

____

8. Ne retournez pas après 22h00 dimanche soir!

____

7 At the beginning of the school year, teachers have specific instructions for what you need to do to be successful in their courses and in school in general. Write out their suggestions, beginning each sentence with **Il faut** or **Il ne faut pas**.

Modèle: *Il faut toujours faire les devoirs.*

____

____

____

____

____

____

____

____

Leçon B

8 Find and circle the names of six facial features in French.

O	A	F	S	J	S
R	J	L	L	T	N
E	V	I	N	E	Z
I	Y	E	U	X	U
L	D	O	F	E	P
L	M	S	U	A	L
E	D	N	C	E	X
H	V	E	Z	J	F
C	S	X	S	V	X
U	F	K	S	U	M
O	O	I	V	P	V
B	N	I	H	L	G

9 Label each of the indicated facial features, beginning with **le**, **la**, **l'** or **les**.

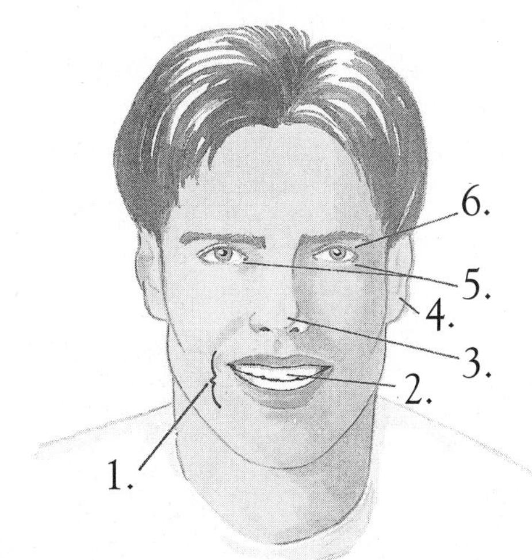

1. ____________________
2. ____________________
3. ____________________
4. ____________________
5. ____________________
6. ____________________

10 Complete each sentence of the short conversations with the most appropriate expression from the list. Use each choice only once.

quelqu'un	personne	toujours	rien
quelque chose	SOUVENT	jamais	PLUS

1. — Qui parle? Il y a ________________________ dans le garage?

   — Non, il n'y a ________________________.

2. — Est-ce que Michael Jordan joue ________________________ au basket?

   — Non, il ne joue ________________________ au basket.

3. — Tu as ________________________ dans la bouche?

   — Non, maman. Je n'ai ________________________ dans la bouche.

4. — Il pleut ________________________ à Seattle.

   — C'est vrai. Mais dans le désert il ne pleut ________________________.

POUR TOI

Verbs + infinitives

Certain French verbs may be followed directly by an infinitive:

adorer	désirer	préférer
aimer	falloir	venir
aller	pouvoir	vouloir

Je **vais étudier** avec des amis ce soir.

Veux-tu **venir** chez moi à 19h00?

11 Waiting for class to begin, Philippe listens to what some of his classmates are saying. Complete each of their sentences with the appropriate form of one of the listed verbs. Make sure to use each verb at least once.

aimer falloir pouvoir
vouloir aller venir préférer

1. — Frédéric, tu ________________ aller au cinéma avec moi samedi soir?
   — Samedi soir? Je ne ________________ pas aller au cinéma avec toi parce que je vais sortir avec Sylvie.
2. — Tiens, Joséphine! Tu ________________ être professeur ou journaliste?
   — Je ________________ être journaliste.
3. — Est-ce que tu ________________ skier en hiver?
   — Non, pas beaucoup. Il fait trop froid.
4. — Qu'est-ce que tu ________________ faire après les cours?
   — Mes amis ________________ chez moi jouer aux jeux vidéo.
5. — En cours il ________________ parler français.
   — Voilà le prof qui arrive! Parlons français!
6. — Est-ce que vous ________________ manger à la cantine ou au fast-food?
   — Moi, je ________________ manger au fast-food.

12 As practice for writing to your French-speaking pen pal, tell what you like, don't like, want, don't want, and are going to do by completing each sentence with an infinitive phrase. You can choose completions from the list, or you can use others that you have already learned.

jouer au basket	**aller au centre commercial**	**faire du roller**
parler français	**faire les magasins**	**jouer aux jeux vidéo**
sortir avec des amis	**étudier à la maison**	**acheter de la glace**
préparer les repas	**manger au fast-food**	

Modèle: J'adore....
J'adore aller au cinéma le samedi.

1. Je veux.... ______________________________
2. Je ne veux pas.... ______________________________
3. J'aime.... ______________________________
4. Je n'aime pas.... ______________________________
5. J'adore.... ______________________________
6. Je préfère.... ______________________________
7. Je vais.... ______________________________

13 Now write a short letter to this French-speaking pen pal using four of the sentences that you composed in Activity 12. After each of your sentences, ask your pen pal a related question.

Modèle: *Je veux voyager en France cet été.*
Et toi, est-ce que tu veux voyager aux États-Unis un jour?

____

____

____

____

____

____

POUR TOI

Negative expressions

Here are some negative expressions that follow the same pattern as **ne (n')... pas**:

Affirmative	Negative
souvent (*often*) **toujours** (*always*)	**ne (n')... jamais** (*never*)
toujours (*still*)	**ne (n')... plus** (*no longer, not anymore*)
quelqu'un (*someone, somebody*)	**ne (n')... personne** (*no one, nobody, not anyone*)
quelque chose (*something*)	**ne (n')... rien** (*nothing, not anything*)

Solange parle **toujours** français. Elle **ne** parle **jamais** anglais.

Il y a **quelqu'un** au téléphone. Il **n'**y a **personne** à la porte.

Je prends **quelque chose** à manger. Mon demi-frère **ne** prend **rien**.

14 Rearrange the following words to make logical sentences.

1. toujours/frère/dents/mon/a/aux/mal

2. les/quelqu'un/cours/attends/après/j'

3. de/plus/tu/roller/fais/ne

4. son/voulons/chose/nous/quelque/anniversaire/pour/acheter

____

5. centre/Maxine/rien/commercial/au/ne/trouve

____

6. soir/font/ces/jamais/ne/élèves/vendredi/devoirs/leurs

____

7. cinéma/il/soir/a/au/personne/y/n'/ce

____

8. arrivent/le/tantes/ses/après/toujours/dessert

____

9. souvent/maison/la/Henri/à/étudie

____

15 Match each question with the letter of the most appropriate answer.

_____ 1. Fais-tu toujours tes devoirs?

_____ 2. Téléphones-tu à Cécile ce soir?

_____ 3. Joues-tu toujours aux jeux vidéo?

_____ 4. Veux-tu quelque chose à manger?

_____ 5. Attends-tu quelqu'un au centre commercial?

_____ 6. Écoutes-tu toujours le reggae?

A. Non, je n'attends personne.

B. Non, je ne joue plus à ces jeux.

C. Non, je n'écoute jamais cette musique.

D. Non, je ne vais parler à personne.

E. Non, je ne fais jamais mes devoirs le weekend.

F. Non, je ne prends rien. Je n'ai pas faim.

16 Rewrite each sentence, adding the appropriate negative expression and making any other necessary changes.

Modèle: (ne... jamais) Les élèves en France vont à l'école le mercredi après-midi.
Les élèves en France ne vont jamais à l'école le mercredi après-midi.

1. (ne... plus) Mes amis jouent au foot.

____

2. (ne... rien) Nous faisons nos devoirs de maths.

____

3. (ne... jamais) Jean-Pierre et moi, nous prenons le petit déjeuner le matin.

____

4. (ne... personne) Le professeur parle à Fabrice après les cours.

____

5. (ne... plus) Tu regardes la télé le samedi matin.

____

6. (n'... rien) Maman achète des légumes au marché.

____

7. (ne... jamais) On skie en juillet.

____

8. (ne... personne) Il y a quelqu'un dans la cuisine.

____

17 Answer the following questions.

1. Tu parles toujours anglais en cours de français?

 ____

2. Tu achètes quelque chose à manger à la cantine aujourd'hui?

 ____

3. Tu finis toujours à deux heures?

 ____

4. Tu attends quelqu'un après les cours?

 ____

5. Tu vas toujours au fast-food après les cours?

 ____

6. Tu parles souvent français à la maison?

 ____

7. Tu as toujours peur de prendre rendez-vous avec le/la dentiste?

 ____

8. Tu portes un short en hiver?

 ____

Leçon C

18 Complete the crossword puzzle with the French words that describe how someone is feeling.

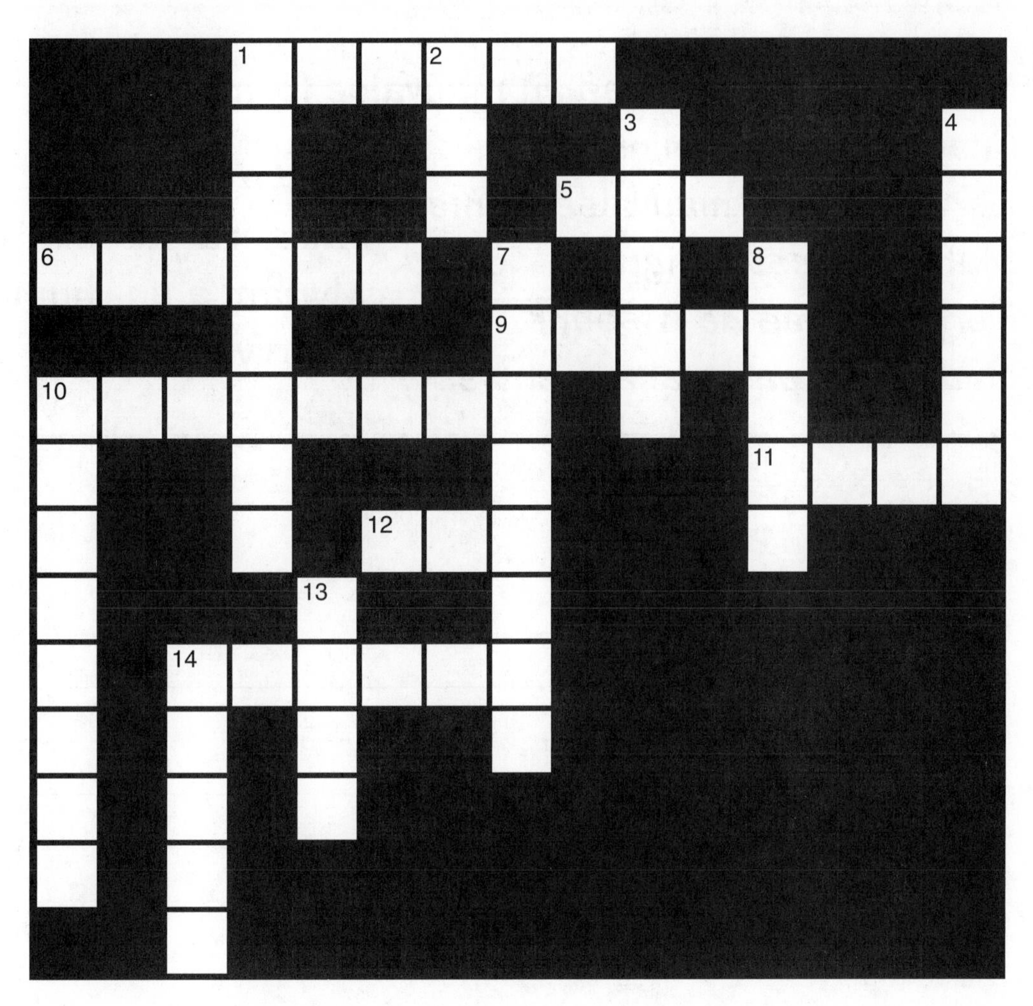

Across

1. Oh là là! Maurice ne va pas bien. Il est....
5. Étienne a beaucoup de livres dans son sac à dos. Il a mal au....
6. Gérard a chaud. Il a de la....
9. Atchoum! Mme Garnier a un....
10. Sara travaille beaucoup. Elle est toujours....
11. Quand mon grand-père écoute le rock, il a mal à la....
12. Le médecin demande, "Où as-tu...?"
14. Thérèse ne veut pas manger. Elle a la....

Down

1. Ça va mal. J'ai... mine.
2. David a mal... dents.
3. Je ne veux pas manger. J'ai mal au....
4. Ils mangent trop de desserts. Donc, ils ont mal au....
7. Les petits enfants ont souvent mal aux....
8. Les enfants mangent trop de sucre. Donc, ils ont mal aux....
10. Véro a froid et elle a des....
13. Ça va bien. J'ai bonne....
14. Quand Suzanne a mal à la..., elle veut manger de la glace.

19 Decide if the people listed below are healthy or not. Copy each sentence, putting it in the appropriate category.

Mlle Fournier n'est pas en mauvaise forme.
Charles a bonne mine.
Karima est en mauvaise forme.
Mahmoud est fatigué.
Hervé n'a pas de frissons.
Nadine n'a pas mal au ventre.
Théo a la grippe.
Zakia n'a pas mal au cœur.
Myriam a un rhume.
Thierry a mal à la gorge.

En bonne santé

____
____
____
____
____
____
____
____

En mauvaise santé

____
____
____
____
____
____
____
____

20 Complete each sentence of the short conversations with the most appropriate expression from the list. Use each choice only once.

ventre	mine	fièvre	fatigué	RHUME	épaules
forme	grippe	gorge	dos	malade	frissons

1. — Je fais beaucoup d'exercices. Donc, je suis en bonne ________________.
   — Alors, tu n'es pas trop ________________?
2. — Daniel ne veut rien manger. Il a la ________________.
   — Est-ce qu'il a mal au ________________?
   — Oui, et il a aussi de la ________________.
3. — Christiane a toujours bonne ________________.
   — Oui, elle n'est jamais ________________.
4. — Oh là là! J'ai froid et j'ai des ________________.
   — As-tu un ________________?
5. — Il a trop de livres dans son sac à dos et maintenant il a mal au ________.
   — A-t-il aussi mal aux ________________?
6. — Pourquoi Laurent ne peut-il pas parler?
   — Il a un chat dans la ________________.

21 For each complaint, write the letter of the most logical suggestion. Use each suggestion only once.

_____ 1. J'ai mal aux jambes.
_____ 2. J'ai la grippe.
_____ 3. J'ai mal aux bras.
_____ 4. J'ai mal aux dents.
_____ 5. J'ai mal au dos.
_____ 6. J'ai mal à la gorge.
_____ 7. J'ai mal au cœur.
_____ 8. J'ai mal aux oreilles.

A. Ne faites pas de vélo!
B. N'écoutez pas tant (*so much*) le rock!
C. Ne mettez pas tant de livres dans votre sac à dos!
D. Ne faites pas de roller quand il pleut!
E. Restez au lit!
F. Ne mangez pas tant de pommes vertes!
G. Ne faites pas d'aérobic!
H. Ne mangez pas tant de sucre!

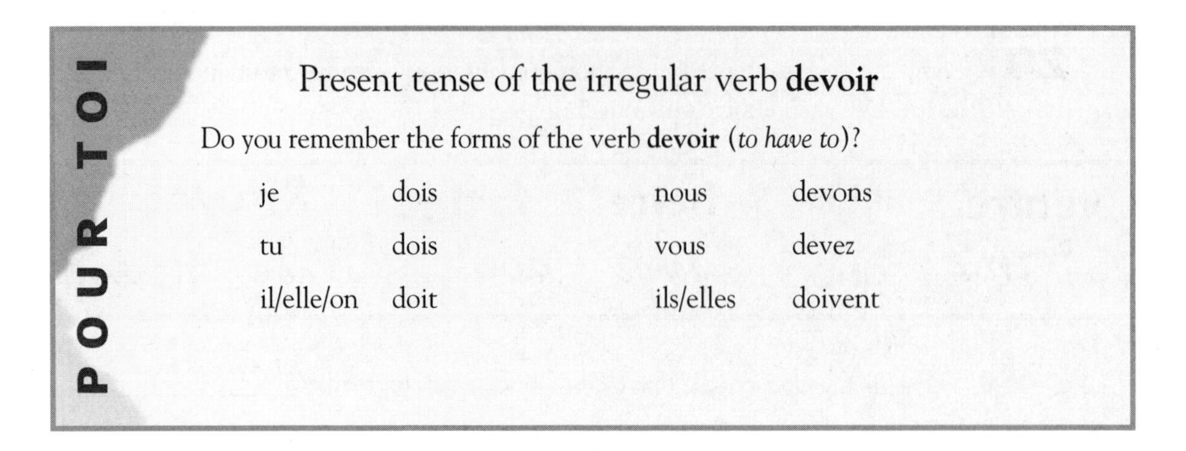

POUR TOI

Present tense of the irregular verb **devoir**

Do you remember the forms of the verb **devoir** (*to have to*)?

je	dois	nous	devons
tu	dois	vous	devez
il/elle/on	doit	ils/elles	doivent

22 Match what the following people have to do with the letter of what they must do to accomplish this.

_____ 1. Francine doit nager.

_____ 2. Vous devez manger un sandwich à midi.

_____ 3. Cécile et Sabrina doivent regarder cette vidéo.

_____ 4. Je dois acheter des choses pour préparer le dîner.

_____ 5. Oh là là! Édouard doit avoir mal au ventre!

_____ 6. Tu dois acheter un nouveau costume pour Noël.

_____ 7. Mr. Johnson doit travailler en France.

_____ 8. Nous devons mettre la table.

A. Il faut aller au supermarché.

B. Il faut aller au centre commercial.

C. Il faut aller à l'océan.

D. Il faut prendre rendez-vous avec le médecin.

E. Il faut trouver le magnétoscope.

F. Il faut prendre la nappe, les serviettes et les cuillers.

G. Il faut commencer à étudier le français.

H. Il faut trouver du pain, du fromage et du jambon.

23

Denis wants to go on a picnic this weekend, but everyone he asks has something else they have to do. Tell what it is by completing their sentences with the appropriate form of the verb **devoir**.

1. Nous regrettons, Denis, mais nous ____________________ aller chez nos grands-parents.
2. Je regrette, Denis, mais je ____________________ faire du shopping avec ma sœur.
3. C'est dommage (*too bad*)! Nicolas et moi, nous ____________________ rester à la maison pour aider nos parents.
4. Je regrette, Denis. Je ____________________ faire les courses pour ma mère.
5. Dommage! Nous ne pouvons pas parce que nous ____________________ faire du camping avec la famille.
6. Je regrette, mais je ____________________ prendre rendez-vous avec le dentiste.
7. Mais, Denis, Normand et toi, vous ____________________ travailler à 11h00 samedi!
8. Et Denis, tu ____________________ faire tes devoirs dimanche!

24

Alain looks around his classroom and notes how many old things ought to be replaced with new ones. Write out what he tells his classmates.

Modèle: Pierre et toi, vous avez un vieux dictionnaire.
Pierre et toi, vous devez acheter un nouveau dictionnaire.

1. Ousmane et Salim ont de vieux cahiers.

   ____

2. Tu as une vieille disquette.

   ____

3. Monique a de vieux crayons.

   ____

4. Zohra et toi, vous avez de vieilles cassettes.

   ____

5. Paul a un vieux calendrier.

   ____

6. La prof a un vieil ordinateur.

____

7. Nous avons de vieux sacs à dos.

____

8. Moi, j'ai une vieille troussse.

____

25 Answer the following questions.

1. À quelle heure est-ce que tu dois arriver à l'école?

____

2. Avec qui est-ce que tu dois parler français?

____

3. Quand est-ce que tu dois faire tes devoirs?

____

4. Est-ce que tu dois aller à l'école le samedi matin?

____

5. Est-ce que tu dois travailler à la maison?

____

6. À quelle heure est-ce que tu dois retourner à la maison vendredi soir?

____

7. Quand est-ce que tu dois prendre rendez-vous avec le/la dentiste?

____

8. Quand est-ce que tu dois rester au lit?

____

Unité 11 En vacances

Leçon A

1 Complete the crossword puzzle with the French names of the indicated countries and nationalities.

Across

4. Frédéric est luxembourgeois; il vient du....
5. Thierry est belge; il vient de....
7. Katia vient du Luxembourg; elle est....
8. Vivianne est française; elle vient de....

Down

1. Marc est de Luxembourg; il est....
2. Jérôme vient de Belgique; il est....
3. Carole est suisse; elle vient de....
6. Ingrid est européenne; elle vient d'....

2 Based on where the following people live, identify their nationality.

Modèle: Marie-Laure habite à Paris.
Elle est française.

1. Éric habite à Bruxelles. ______________________________
2. Mlle Berthelot habite à Luxembourg. ______________________________
3. Isabelle et Marie-Thérèse habitent à Genève. ______________________________
4. Suzanne et son mari habitent à Bruxelles. ______________________________
5. Mme Debroas et sa fille habitent à Tours. ______________________________
6. Nicolas et sa sœur habitent à Luxembourg. ______________________________
7. M. Garrigues habite à Lausanne. ______________________________
8. M. et Mme Ger habitent à Chamonix. ______________________________

3 Depending on their nationality, tell what country the following people come from.

Modèle: Les Delmas sont français; ils viennent de *France*.

1. Luis Herrera et sa femme sont mexicains; ils viennent du ______________________.
2. Michiko est japonaise; elle vient du ______________________.
3. Sal est italien; il vient d'______________________.
4. M. Li est chinois; il vient de ______________________.
5. Martina et son frère sont allemands; ils viennent d'______________________.
6. Karine est luxembourgeoise; elle vient du ______________________.
7. John est américain; il vient des ______________________.
8. M. et Mme Martínez sont espagnols; ils viennent d'______________________.
9. Paul est belge; il vient de ______________________.
10. Odile et ses frères sont suisses; ils viennent de ______________________.

POUR TOI

Passé composé with être

The **passé composé** is a past tense that is composed of two verbs: the appropriate present tense form of **être** and the past participle of the main verb. The past participle of an **-er** verb changes the infinitive ending to **é**. The past participle of an **-ir** verb changes the infinitive ending to **i** or **u**.

Nous **sommes partis** pour Bruxelles. *We left for Brussels.*

Here are some verbs that use the helping verb **être**, along with their past participles.

Infinitive	Past Participle
all**er**	all**é**
arriv**er**	arriv**é**
entr**er**	entr**é**
rentr**er**	rentr**é**
rest**er**	rest**é**
part**ir**	part**i**
sort**ir**	sort**i**
ven**ir**	ven**u**

Note that the past participle of the verb agrees in gender and in number with the subject.

arriver

je	suis	arrivé(e)	nous	sommes	arrivé(e)s
tu	es	arrivé(e)	vous	êtes	arrivé(e)(s)(es)
il/on	est	arrivé	ils	sont	arrivés
elle	est	arrivée	elles	sont	arrivées

POUR TOI

To form a negative sentence in the **passé composé**, put **ne (n')** before the form of **être** and **pas** after it.

Mon frère **n'**est **pas** allé à la gare.

To form a question in the **passé composé** using inversion, put the subject pronoun after the form of **être**.

Mireille, pourquoi **es-tu partie**?

4 On Monique's first day working at a popular boutique, many of her friends and family stopped by. At school on Monday, she talks about everyone who came in. Complete her sentences with the appropriate **passé composé** form of the verb **venir**.

Modèle: Ma mère *est venue* pour acheter un cadeau d'anniversaire.

1. Nathalie et Francine ____________________ pour acheter des chaussettes.
2. Amélie et toi, Myriam, vous ____________________... euh, pour parler!
3. Après le film Bénédicte ____________________ avec sa sœur pour acheter une chemise.
4. Nicole et Olivier ____________________ pour regarder des vêtements d'été.
5. Mon professeur d'anglais ____________________ pour chercher un pull.
6. Élisabeth, tu ____________________ pour regarder le garçon qui travaille avec moi, n'est-ce pas?
7. Mohamed et son père ____________________ pour chercher un costume.
8. Et Pierre? Pourquoi est-ce que tu ____________________?

5 Tell what everyone did this past weekend. Complete each sentence with the appropriate **passé composé** form of the indicated verb.

1. (sortir) Mes sœurs ________________________ avec leurs amis.
2. (rentrer) Max et moi, nous ________________________ après nos vacances en Suisse.
3. (rester) Dimanche je ________________________ à la maison pour étudier.
4. (venir) Les frères Kraft ________________________ d'Allemagne.
5. (partir) La sœur de Philippe ________________________ pour la Belgique.
6. (aller) Dhamel et toi, vous ________________________ au centre commercial pour acheter des shorts.
7. (arriver) Mme Sarlais ________________________ au Luxembourg pour voir ses parents.
8. (entrer) Et toi, Vivianne, est-ce que tu ________________________ dans la nouvelle boutique?

6 Complete a paragraph in Isabelle's diary by writing the appropriate **passé composé** forms of the indicated verbs.

Ce weekend ma sœur Yvette ________________________ (venir) de Bordeaux. Elle ________________________ (arriver) à la maison vendredi soir. Elle ________________________ (entrer) quand je parlais au téléphone. Mon père ________________________ (rentrer) cinq minutes après. Puis mon père, ma sœur et moi, nous ________________________ (aller) au restaurant. Samedi soir Yvette et son ami, Laurent, ________________________ (sortir) après le dîner. Dimanche ma sœur et moi, nous ________________________ (rester) à la maison pour regarder la télé. Dimanche soir elle ________________________ (partir) pour Bordeaux à 20h00.

7 During spring break no one from school did what they normally do. Write negative sentences in the **passé composé** to tell what they didn't do.

Modèle: les professeurs/aller à l'école
Les professeurs ne sont pas allés à l'école.

1. Charles, tu/partir pour prendre le bus à 7h00 le matin

   ____

2. Latifa et Anne, vous/sortir de la maison à 7h30

   ____

3. nous/arriver en cours à 8h00

   ____

4. Anne et Claire/venir à la cantine

   ____

5. Stéphanie/entrer dans le fast-food à midi

   ____

6. je/aller étudier avec mes amis

   ____

7. Alexandre/rentrer à 20h00

   ____

8. David et Louis/rester à la maison jeudi soir

   ____

8 Using inversion, ask some of your friends what they did last night.

Modèles: Sabrina/sortir avec Paul
Sabrina es-tu sortie avec Paul?

Robert et Fabrice/aller en boîte
Robert et Fabrice êtes-vous allés en boîte?

1. Laïla et Karine/rester à la maison pour regarder la télé

   ____

2. Jean-François/rentrer de vacances

   ____

3. Assane/aller au cinéma

____

4. Jean et Pierre/partir avec Thierry

____

5. Michèle et Françoise/arriver à la maison à minuit

____

6. Arabéa/sortir avec tes parents

____

7. Sophie/venir à la boum

____

8. Robert et Malika/entrer dans le fast-food

____

9 Answer the following questions about what you did last weekend.

1. Est-ce que tu es sorti(e) avec tes amis?

____

2. Est-ce que tu es allé(e) au cinéma?

____

3. Est-ce que tu es rentré(e) après minuit vendredi soir?

____

4. Est-ce que tu es parti(e) pour faire du shopping samedi après-midi?

____

5. Est-ce que tu es entré(e) dans un magasin?

____

6. Est-ce que ton ami(e) est venu(e) chez toi?

____

7. Est-ce que tu es resté(e) à la maison dimanche soir?

____

Leçon B

10 Complete the crossword puzzle with the French names of the indicated African countries and nationalities.

Across

1. Lamine est congolaise; elle vient de République Démocratique du....
7. Amine vient de Tunisie; il est....
8. Fatima est ivoirienne; elle vient de....
9. Arabéa est algérienne; elle vient d'....

Down

1. Nora vient de République Démocratique du Congo; elle est....
2. Jamila vient d'Algérie; elle est....
3. Yasmine vient de Tunisie; elle est....
4. Djamel vient de Côte d'Ivoire; il est....
5. Adja vient du Sénégal; elle est....
6. Fayçal est marocain; il vient du....

11 Based on their nationality, tell where the following people live.

Modèle: M. Daho est algérien; il habite en *Algérie*.

1. Nicolas est luxembourgeois; il habite au ______________________.
2. Mme Zoubia est ivoirienne; elle habite en ______________________.
3. M. Diouf est sénégalais; il habite au ______________________.
4. Aïcha est tunisienne; elle habite en ______________________.
5. Dikembe est marocain; il habite au ______________________.
6. Khadim et Ousmane sont africains; ils habitent en ______________________.
7. Alex est belge; il habite en ______________________.

POUR TOI

Ordinal numbers

To form most ordinal numbers in French, add **-ième** to the cardinal number. If a cardinal number ends in **-e**, drop the **-e** before adding **-ième**. Note that there are a few irregular ordinal numbers.

1er, 1ère = premier, première	6e = sixième
2e = deuxième	7e = septième
3e = troisième	8e = huitième
4e = quatrième	9e = neuvième
5e = cinquième	10e = dixième

12 Unscramble the letters of the following ordinal numbers.

1. èumnivee

   ____

2. irèemtauq

   ____

3. xmèeiid

   ____

4. rmeripe

   ____

5. pemitèes

____

6. oesimèrit

____

7. umèiethi

____

8. nueècmiqi

____

13

Tell how certain women placed in a recent marathon.

Modèle: Marie Dumont/6^{e}
Marie Dumont est la sixième.

1. Paola Caprioli/4e ______________________________
2. Thérèse Milo/5e ______________________________
3. Karine Renaudet/2e ______________________________
4. Isabelle Paganelli/7e ______________________________
5. Andrée Riva/9e ______________________________
6. Sonia Poitras/3e ______________________________
7. Gabrielle Blondel/1ère ______________________________
8. Delphine Lannion/8e ______________________________

14 Imagine that your job at the *Tour de France* is to announce the order of bikers as they cross the finish line in Paris. Give the nationalities of the top nine bikers as they finish the race. (You may need to refer to page 382 in your textbook for help with each country's flag.) The first-place winner has been done for you as a model.

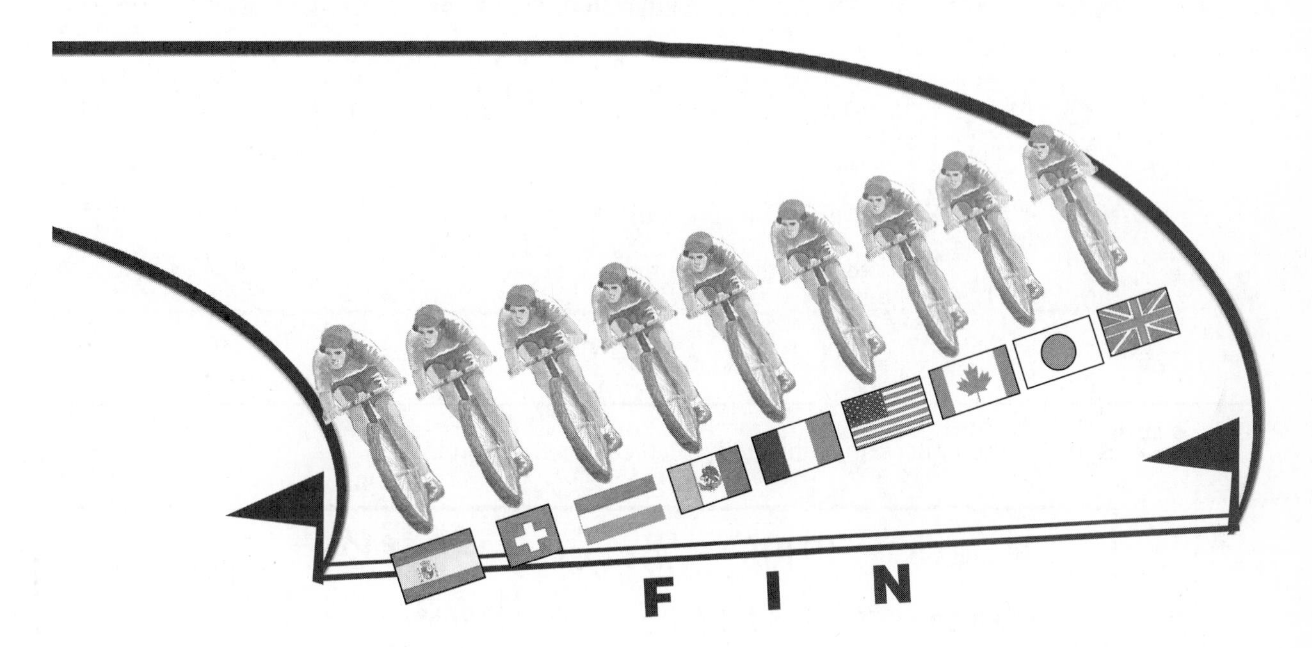

Modèle: *L'Espagnol est le premier.*

____

____

____

____

____

____

____

____

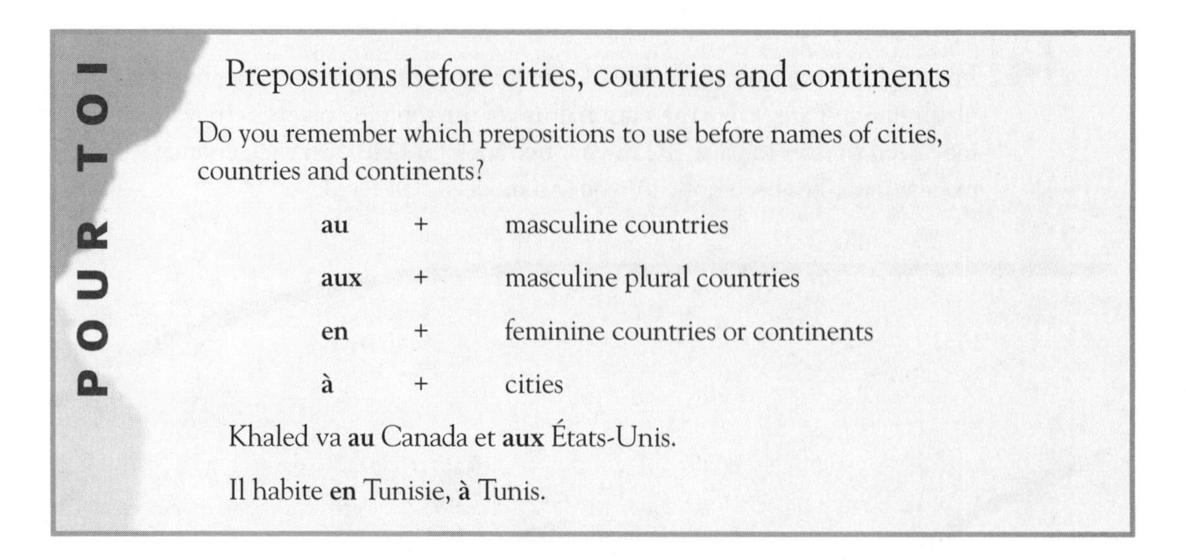

POUR TOI

Prepositions before cities, countries and continents

Do you remember which prepositions to use before names of cities, countries and continents?

au	+	masculine countries
aux	+	masculine plural countries
en	+	feminine countries or continents
à	+	cities

Khaled va **au** Canada et **aux** États-Unis.

Il habite **en** Tunisie, **à** Tunis.

15 Based on his or her nationality, tell which city each person lives in.

Rome PARIS Berlin Genève Abidjan
Orlando BRUXELLES Madrid Dakar

Modèle: Mme Graf est allemande.
Elle habite à Berlin.

1. M. Fernández est espagnol.

____

2. Mme Torti est sénégalaise.

____

3. Mlle Lapougeas est française.

____

4. M. Pau est belge.

____

5. Mlle Caprioli est italienne.

____

6. M. Ledoux est suisse.

___

7. Mme Koster est américaine.

___

8. M. Yondo est ivoirien.

___

16 Although most countries have a cultural mix of people from many places, the majority of their residents have lived there for many generations. Write French sentences that express this idea.

Modèle: la France
En France il y a beaucoup de Français.

1. la Tunisie

___

2. le Sénégal

___

3. le Maroc

___

4. la Belgique

___

5. les États-Unis

___

6. l'Algérie

___

7. le Canada

___

8. la Côte-d'Ivoire

___

17 Brenda has written a composition about some of her friends who come from other countries. Complete her sentences with **à**, **au**, **en** or **aux**.

J'ai beaucoup d'amis qui ne sont pas américains. Nathalie habite ________________ Genève. Cette ville, qui est ________________ Suisse, est très belle. Max et sa famille habitent ________________ Canada. Je vais souvent ________________ Montréal pour visiter leur ville. Carole voyage souvent ________________ Côte-d'Ivoire parce que son ami et sa famille habitent ________________ Abidjan, la ville principale. Ahmed habite ________________ Algers, qui est ________________ Algérie. Cette ville a une histoire intéressante. Et moi? J'habite ________________ États-Unis, ________________ Chicago.

Leçon C

18 Find and circle the French names of 14 buildings or places in or near the city.

B	M	U	S	É	E	O	V	E	H	B	E	E	I	P
I	W	B	M	T	N	M	K	U	R	S	X	U	Q	Q
B	E	C	E	A	A	A	J	Z	C	H	Q	H	B	F
L	N	U	A	N	I	D	X	K	D	F	L	K	B	N
I	Q	W	Q	B	I	R	E	K	C	S	I	H	E	X
O	P	E	R	N	A	C	I	D	R	K	E	T	E	V
T	N	A	R	U	A	T	S	E	R	O	S	V	A	G
H	Q	V	E	L	T	B	M	I	G	O	U	Y	J	R
È	C	T	P	É	G	B	C	V	P	A	B	B	P	Y
Q	E	T	O	X	G	T	T	L	X	R	L	D	A	K
U	N	B	V	Y	B	L	V	O	M	O	Q	P	Q	F
E	I	R	I	A	R	B	I	L	F	K	Q	X	X	U
N	A	S	Q	C	J	O	E	S	K	C	O	G	Z	H
Z	E	B	A	W	C	G	G	Z	E	O	H	R	E	I

19 Complete the crossword puzzle with the French expressions for buildings or places in or near the city and what you can find there.

Across

1. On achète des livres à la....
4. On peut acheter des... de voyage à la banque.
8. On peut lire des livres à la....
9. On peut nager dans une piscine ou dans la....
10. On trouve Monsieur le Maire à la....
11. On trouve beaucoup d'... à la banque.
14. On va à l'... le dimanche.
15. À la mer on peut nager ou rester sur la....

Down

2. On dîne au....
3. Notre école a une... où les élèves peuvent nager.
5. On trouve beaucoup d'argent à la....
6. On achète des... au tabac ou à la poste.
7. On fait du sport au....
9. On trouve des sculptures au....
12. On peut acheter des timbres à la poste ou au....
13. Au centre de la ville, il y a souvent une....

20

Complete each sentence with the letter that describes what you can do at that place.

_____ 1. Au stade...	A. nous achetons des timbres.
_____ 2. À la piscine...	B. on regarde les objets d'art.
_____ 3. À la banque...	C. on prend des repas.
_____ 4. À la poste...	D. nous jouons au foot.
_____ 5. À la bibliothèque...	E. les élèves étudient et font leurs devoirs.
_____ 6. Au musée...	F. on peut acheter des livres.
_____ 7. À la librairie...	G. mon père et ma mère gardent leur argent.
_____ 8. Au restaurant...	H. ma sœur nage après les cours.

21

Tell where the following places are located in relation to your house by completing the sentences with **au nord**, **à l'est**, **au sud** or **à l'ouest**.

1. Mon école est ________________________________ de chez moi.
2. La bibliothèque est ____________________________ de chez moi.
3. La poste est ____________________________ de chez moi.
4. Le stade est ____________________________ de chez moi.
5. La mairie est ____________________________ de chez moi.
6. Mon église est ____________________________ de chez moi.
7. La banque est ____________________________ de chez moi.
8. La piscine est ____________________________ de chez moi.

22 Draw a map of your neighborhood. Include the following places and label them in French.

ma maison	**la bibliothèque**	**la poste**
le stade	**la banque**	**mon église**
le restaurant	**la piscine**	**mon école**

23 Using the drawing you created in Activity 22, tell where each place you identified is located in relation to another one. Use **à gauche de, à droite de, près de** or **loin de**.

Modèle: *La poste est près de la banque.*

____

____

____

____

____

____

____

____

____

POUR TOI

Present tense of the irregular verb **voir**

Do you remember the forms of the verb **voir** (*to see*)?

je	vois	nous	voyons
tu	vois	vous	voyez
il/elle/on	voit	ils/elles	voient

24 Francine and many of her classmates and neighbors are attending the school concert. Tell whom or what they see there, completing each of Francine's sentences with the appropriate form of the verb **voir**.

1. Marlène et sa mère ____________________ le professeur de musique.
2. Je ____________________ mon ami Vincent qui joue du violon.
3. M. et Mme Fratellini ____________________ leurs parents.
4. Mon père et moi, nous ____________________ la famille Senghor.
5. Tu ____________________ le nouveau piano de l'école.

6. Delphine et toi, vous ________________________ les élèves de musique.
7. Nadia ________________________ son professeur de maths et sa femme.
8. Après le concert Guillaume ________________________ les desserts!

---

25 Answer the following questions.

1. Qui voit le professeur dans la salle de classe?

   ____

2. Où est-ce que les élèves voient les professeurs?

   ____

3. Qu'est-ce qu'on voit dans une librairie?

   ____

4. Où est-ce que tu vois tes amis?

   ____

5. Où est-ce qu'on voit les films?

   ____

6. Quand est-ce que tu vois tes parents?

   ____

7. Qui est-ce que tu vois le jour de ton anniversaire?

   ____

8. Qui est-ce que tu vois quand tu es malade?

   ____

Unité 12 À Paris

Leçon A

1 In the grid that follows, find nine French expressions that are related to the Parisian subway system. (You may want to refer to pages 406, 409 and 410 in your textbook.)

C	X	F	D	R	A	Q	T	C	D	K	J	K	Q
O	R	T	É	M	E	E	A	U	N	B	R	B	R
R	B	G	N	K	H	R	O	B	J	G	X	S	K
R	Y	Q	O	C	N	X	I	L	U	Q	M	R	W
E	K	S	I	E	A	L	C	D	D	X	M	I	I
S	V	U	T	D	L	R	A	R	D	A	K	U	T
P	G	A	A	E	I	D	Z	Z	J	H	W	H	T
O	O	A	T	X	J	K	T	B	U	U	V	Q	I
N	B	R	S	Z	F	Q	E	F	O	V	W	S	V
D	I	E	T	Q	W	G	G	V	A	K	L	P	F
A	F	D	A	E	W	S	M	V	M	P	D	N	C
N	A	L	P	R	S	E	Y	R	K	V	U	Q	W
C	O	F	H	Y	C	J	I	G	H	Z	R	H	F
E	K	I	M	Z	P	C	N	D	J	C	H	P	G

2 Complete the crossword puzzle with the new French words from this lesson.

Across

1. Il y a plus de 300 stations de... à Paris.
4. Karine a perdu son... de métro.
5. Il faut aller au... pour acheter un billet de métro.
6. Cet... est très grand. Il a 400 chambres.
7. On trouve beaucoup de tombeaux au....
8. *La Joconde* est un... de Léonard de Vinci.
9. On peut acheter un billet de métro dans une... de métro.
11. Quand on prend un... sur la Seine, on peut bien voir que Paris est la "Ville lumière."
12. Les... des Tuileries sont très beaux.

Down

1. La tour Eiffel est un... célèbre de Paris.
2. Il y a dix... dans un carnet.
3. À Paris il y a une petite... de la Liberté.
10. Le... de Jim Morrison est au cimetière du Père-Lachaise.

Passé composé with avoir

POUR TOI

In the last unit you learned that some French verbs form their **passé composé** with the helping verb **être**. But most French verbs use the helping verb **avoir** and the past participle of the main verb. Past participles of **-er** verbs change the infinitive ending to **é**. Past participles of most **-ir** verbs change the infinitive ending to **i**, and most **-re** verbs change the infinitive ending to **u**.

Michelle **a quitté** l'hôtel à 9h00. *Michelle left the hotel at 9:00.*

Note that the past participle of the verb does not agree with the subject.

demander

j'	ai	demandé	nous	avons	demandé
tu	as	demandé	vous	avez	demandé
il/elle/on	a	demandé	ils/elles	ont	demandé

To form a negative sentence in the **passé composé**, put **n'** before the form of **avoir** and **pas** after it.

Vous **n'**avez **pas** fini vos devoirs.

To form a question in the **passé composé** using inversion, put the subject pronoun after the form of **avoir**.

Où **as**-tu **attendu** tes amis?

3 Many students have an important history test on Monday, and so they studied over the weekend. Tell when they studied by completing each sentence of their short conversations with the appropriate **passé composé** form of the verb **étudier**.

Modèle: — Marianne? Est-ce que tu *as étudié* vendredi soir chez ton ami?
— Non, j'*ai étudié* samedi matin à l'école.

1. — Sarah et Nadia? Est-ce que vous ______________________________ à l'école aussi?
   — Non, nous ______________________________ à la bibliothèque samedi après-midi.

2. — Moi, j'______________________________ la Révolution française vendredi et l'histoire de Napoléon samedi.
   — Est-ce que tu ______________________________ à la maison ou à la bibliothèque?

3. — Et Jean ______________________________ avec son cousin qui est prof d'histoire, n'est-ce pas?

   — Quelle chance! Ils ______________________________ ensemble dimanche soir.

4. — Les sœurs Dumont, elles ______________________________ dimanche après-midi.

   — Et leur amie Myriam ______________________________ au jardin du Luxembourg parce qu'il faisait si beau.

4 However, not all the students studied for the history test. Complete their explanations of what they did instead. In the first blank, write the appropriate negative **passé composé** form of the verb **étudier**. In the second blank, write the appropriate **passé composé** form of the indicated verb. (Attention: Some of the indicated verbs use **avoir** and some use **être**.)

Modèle: (jouer) Je *n'ai pas étudié* parce que j'*ai joué* au foot.

1. (voyager) Charles et Delphine ______________________________ parce qu'ils ______________________________ en Belgique.
2. (rentrer) Sandrine et moi, nous ______________________________ parce que nous ______________________________ à minuit dimanche soir.
3. (préférer) Sophie et sa cousine ______________________________ parce qu'elles ______________________________ aller au cinéma.
4. (travailler) Tu ______________________________ parce que tu ______________________________ tout le weekend.
5. (rester) Jacqueline et toi, vous ______________________________ parce que vous ______________________________ à la maison de votre grand-mère près de Giverny.
6. (inviter) Je ______________________________ parce que dimanche j'______________________________ des amis à venir chez moi.
7. (garder) Élisabeth ______________________________ parce qu'elle ______________________________ les enfants de son frère.
8. (aller) Paul et Amine ______________________________ parce qu'ils ______________________________ au Louvre avec leurs cousins d'Allemagne.

5 The students at the Lycée St. Louis in Paris recently chose an additional foreign language to begin studying next year. Tell what everyone has selected by writing the appropriate **passé composé** form of the verb **choisir** (*to choose*).

Modèle: Marie-Alix *a choisi* l'espagnol.

1. Max et son amie ______________________________ l'anglais.
2. Serge et toi, vous ______________________________ l'allemand.
3. Philippe ______________________________ le japonais.
4. Jamila et moi, nous ______________________________ l'italien.
5. Les demi-frères de Patricia ______________________________ le latin.
6. J'______________________________ le russe.
7. La sœur de Martine ______________________________ le chinois.
8. Assia, est-ce que tu ______________________________ le grec?

6 You overheard some French tourists talking about how long they had to wait in line before getting in different Parisian museums. Complete each of their comments, using the appropriate **passé composé** form of the verb **attendre**.

Modèle: Vous *avez attendu* une heure au Louvre?

1. Nous ______________________________ seulement cinq minutes au musée Picasso.
2. Paul et son cousin ______________________________ 30 minutes au musée d'Orsay.
3. Patrick et sa femme ______________________________ 45 minutes au Centre Pompidou.
4. Caroline et toi, vous ______________________________ deux minutes au musée Rodin?
5. Sébastien ______________________________ 20 minutes au musée de Cluny.
6. Notre père ______________________________ dix minutes aux Invalides.
7. Et toi? Tu ______________________________ dix minutes au musée Marmottan?
8. Eh bien, moi, j'______________________________ 15 minutes au musée de l'Orangerie.

7 Certain people's weekend plans didn't turn out exactly as they had intended. Tell what happened to the following people, using the appropriate **passé composé** form of each indicated verb. (Attention: Some of the indicated verbs use **avoir** and some use **être**.)

1. (attendre/venir) J'________________________________ une heure devant le café,

   mais mon amie n'________________ pas ________________.

2. (regarder/dormir) Jacques et moi, nous ________________________________ la télé,

   mais Jacques ________________________________ pendant (*during*) le film.

3. (passer/aller) On ________________________________ mon film préféré au

   Gaumont, mais Robert et moi, nous ____________________________ au théâtre.

4. (aller/danser) Catherine et Paul ________________________________ en boîte,

   mais ils n'________________ pas ________________.

5. (commencer/finir) Vous ________________________________ vos devoirs, mais vous

   n'________________ pas ________________.

6. (acheter/décider) Mme Poirier ________________________________ une nouvelle robe

   verte, mais elle ________________________________ de porter sa vieille robe jaune.

7. (partir/entrer) Tu ________________________________ pour le restaurant avec

   Ahmed à 19h00, mais vous ________________________________ dans le restaurant à 21h30.

8. (jouer/perdre) Martina ________________________________ au tennis à Roland

   Garros, mais elle ________________________________.

8 Imagine that you have just returned home from a two-week trip to France. Your classmates are eager to hear about your experiences. Answer their questions.

Modèles: As-tu parlé français?
Oui, j'ai parlé français.

As-tu voyagé en Allemagne?
Non, je n'ai pas voyagé en Allemagne.

1. Es-tu arrivé(e) à Roissy-Charles de Gaulle?

   ____

2. As-tu visité le cimetière du Père-Lachaise?

   ____

3. As-tu regardé des tableaux au Louvre?

   ____

4. As-tu marché sur l'avenue des Champs-Élysées?

   ____

5. Es-tu allé(e) au cinéma pour voir un film français?

   ____

6. As-tu aimé la cuisine française?

   ____

7. As-tu acheté des vêtements français?

   ____

8. Es-tu rentré(e) avec beaucoup de souvenirs?

   ____

9 A French exchange student from Paris will be visiting your class tomorrow. Write six questions that you could ask this student about what he or she has done in Paris. (You may create your sentences with verbs from the list or you may use others that you already know.)

Modèle: *As-tu visité la tour Eiffel?*

visiter le cimetière du Père-Lachaise
marcher de l'arc de triomphe à la place de la Concorde
manger au fast-food
parler anglais avec des Américains
entrer dans le Louvre
aller à Notre-Dame
regarder Paris d'un bateau sur la Seine
danser dans une boîte

____

____

____

____

____

____

____

____

____

Leçon B

10 Unscramble the following vocabulary words introduced in this lesson. Add **un** or **une** to each word, as appropriate.

1. eur ____________________
2. éélifd ____________________
3. eesuncnmii ____________________
4. lab ____________________
5. 'eecrfftudaii ____________________
6. senimcui ____________________

11 Complete Jérémy's letter to his mother by choosing the most appropriate expression from the list to fill each blank.

bal musiciens Champs-Élysées passer
fête FEU D'ARTIFICE rue défilé chargés JUSQU'À

Chère Maman,

Khadim est venu ____________________ une semaine à Paris. Le soir du 13 juillet il y a eu un ____________________ dans la ____________________ près de son hôtel. Les ____________________ ont très bien joué, et nous avons beaucoup dansé ____________________ deux heures du matin. Le 14 juilllet nous avons regardé le ____________________ militaire le long des *(along the)* ____________________. Et le soir nous sommes allés près de la Seine où il y a eu le beau ____________________ de la ____________________ nationale. Deux jours bien ____________________, n'est-ce pas?

Je t'embrasse,
Jérémy

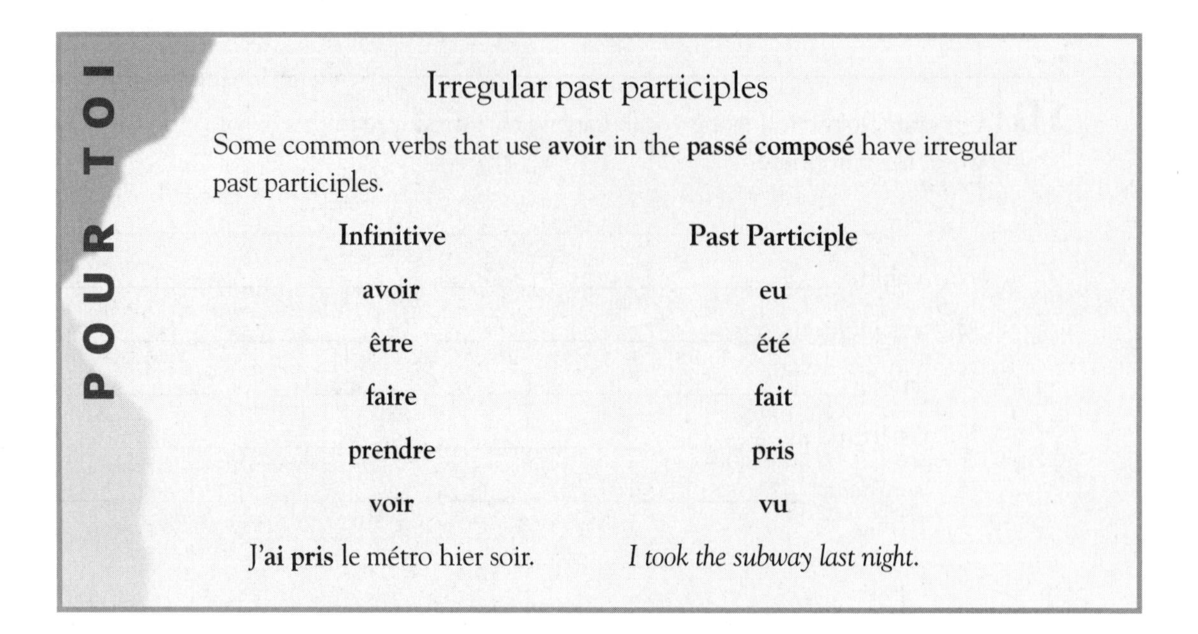

POUR TOI

Irregular past participles

Some common verbs that use **avoir** in the **passé composé** have irregular past participles.

Infinitive	Past Participle
avoir	**eu**
être	**été**
faire	**fait**
prendre	**pris**
voir	**vu**

J'**ai pris** le métro hier soir. *I took the subway last night.*

12 A group of students and several teachers from the Lycée Jules Ferry spent a rainy weekend camping in the mountains. Complete their descriptions of how the group felt after the camping trip. Use the appropriate **passé composé** forms of the verb **avoir**.

Modèle: J'*ai eu* mal à la gorge.

1. Mme Barton, la prof de maths, ________________________ mal à la tête.
2. Richard et son demi-frère ________________________ mal aux jambes.
3. Claude et Françoise, vous ________________________ mal aux épaules.
4. Lucien et moi, nous ________________________ mal aux pieds.
5. Dimanche soir j'________________________ mal au genou.
6. Patrick et la sœur de Catherine ________________________ mal aux bras.
7. Le premier jour Gérard ________________________ mal au cou.
8. Et toi, Manu, tu ________________________ mal au dos.

13 Tell what certain people did during the weekend by writing the most logical expression from the list in the **passé composé**. Use each expression only once.

faire le tour	**faire du camping**	**faire les magasins**
faire un dessert	**faire du baby-sitting**	**faire du roller**
faire du shopping	**faire du vélo**	**faire les devoirs**

Modèle: Marthe est allée au centre commercial où elle *a fait les magasins*.

1. Mme Charbonneau ______________________________ pour sa famille, un beau gâteau au chocolat.
2. Marc et son frère Olivier sont allés dans les Alpes. Ils ______________________________.
3. Mon oncle et ma tante sont allés à Londres. Donc, j'______________________________ pour leurs enfants.
4. David a acheté un nouveau vélo, puis il ______________________________.
5. Thierry et toi, vous êtes sortis avec des amis. Vous ______________________________ près de la tour Eiffel.
6. Nous sommes allés au musée où nous ______________________________.
7. Michel et Antoine ont une interro lundi. Donc, ils ______________________________.
8. Tu es parti à 10h00 pour aller au grand magasin où tu ______________________________.

14 Students on a walking tour of Paris stopped in small groups to have lunch in cafés around the Centre Pompidou. To find out what they had for lunch, complete their short conversations with the appropriate **passé composé** forms of the verb **prendre**.

1. — Malika et moi, nous ______________________________ des sandwichs au jambon.

   — Et qu'est-ce que vous ______________________________ comme boisson?

2. — Michel ______________________________ une omelette et une salade.

   — Et moi, j'______________________________ un hot-dog avec de la moutarde.

3. — Qu'est-ce que tu ______________________________, Thomas?

   — Moi? J'______________________________ une pizza au fromage.

4. — Katia et Myriam ______________________________ des hamburgers au fast-food.

   — Et leurs amies ______________________________ des hamburgers avec des frites.

5. — Madame, qu'est-ce que vous ______________________________?

   — J'______________________________ une salade de tomates et de l'eau minérale.

6. — Aïcha a eu faim. Elle ______________________________ un steak-frites et une glace à la vanille.

   — Et toi, tu ______________________________ un dessert aussi?

15 After this group of students returns home from their trip to France, their family and friends bombard them with questions about what they saw. Complete their short conversations with the appropriate **passé composé** forms of the verb **voir**.

1. — Qu'est-ce que tu ______________________________, Sylvie?

   — Mes amis et moi, nous ______________________________ le beau feu d'artifice du 14 juillet.

2. — Gilbert et toi, est-ce que vous ______________________________ un match de foot?

   — Pas nous, mais Éric et Étienne ______________________________ un match de foot au Parc des Princes.

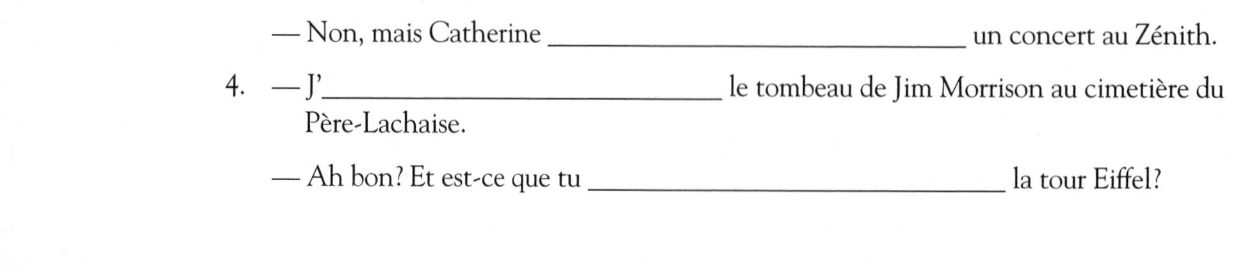

3. — Robert, tu ______________________________ des musiciens français?

   — Non, mais Catherine ______________________________ un concert au Zénith.

4. — J'______________________________ le tombeau de Jim Morrison au cimetière du Père-Lachaise.

   — Ah bon? Et est-ce que tu ______________________________ la tour Eiffel?

5. — Béatrice et toi, vous ______________________________ le Tour de France?

   — Oui, et nous ______________________________ le défilé du 14 juillet aussi.

6. — Les élèves de M. Foster ______________________________ des tableaux impressionnistes au musée d'Orsay?

   — Oui, et ils ______________________________ d'autres tableaux aussi.

16 Complete each sentence with the appropriate **passé composé** form of the most logical verb from the list. Use each verb only once. (Attention: Some of the indicated verbs use **avoir** and some use **être**.)

acheter	avoir	faire	rentrer
voir	aller	ÊTRE	prendre

1. Mes grands-parents ______________________________ un tour en bateau sur la Seine.
2. Tes grands-parents et toi, est-ce que vous ______________________________ la tour Eiffel et beaucoup d'autres monuments parisiens?
3. Tu ______________________________ des photos de Notre-Dame?
4. À une heure du matin M. Vadeboncœur et sa femme ______________________________ du cinéma.
5. Ils ______________________________ obligés de prendre un taxi parce qu'on a fermé le métro.
6. Nadine et moi, nous ______________________________ au concert hier soir.
7. Samedi après-midi j'______________________________ mal au dos après le match de foot.
8. Céline ______________________________ un livre d'Astérix pour son petit frère.

17 Answer the following questions about what you did after school yesterday.

1. Où es-tu allé(e) après les cours?

   ____

2. À quelle heure es-tu rentré(e)?

   ____

3. À qui as-tu téléphoné?

   ____

4. As-tu été obligé(e) de préparer le dîner?

   ____

5. Qu'est-ce que tout le monde a pris?

   ____

6. As-tu fait tes devoirs après le dîner?

   ____

7. Es-tu sorti(e) après le dîner?

   ____

8. As-tu regardé la télé avec ta famille?

   ____

Leçon C

18 Complete the crossword puzzle with names of places in Paris.

Across

3. Le bois de... est à l'est de Paris.
5. On trouve beaucoup d'étudiants dans le... latin de Paris.
7. La... est un quartier moderne au nord-est de Paris.
8. La... des Sciences est un musée moderne.
9. Le Forum des... est un quartier moderne qui a un centre commercial.
11. À la... on peut acheter des CDs et des billets.

Down

1. Le... de Boulogne est à l'ouest de Paris.
2. ... est un quartier artistique de Paris.
4. Le... du Luxembourg est dans le Quartier latin.
6. À la... on peut voir des films.
10. Le Quartier... n'est pas le quartier le plus moderne de Paris.

19

Match the Parisian site with the letter of its description.

_____ 1. le Louvre	A.	un parc au centre de Paris
_____ 2. la Villette	B.	une prison royale qui n'existe pas aujourd'hui
_____ 3. le Forum des Halles	C.	une belle cathédrale
_____ 4. le jardin du Luxembourg	D.	un quartier moderne au centre de Paris
_____ 5. le Centre Pompidou	E.	le musée où l'on peut voir le *Penseur*
_____ 6. les Invalides	F.	le plus grand cimetière de Paris
_____ 7. le musée Rodin	G.	s'appelle aussi "Beaubourg"
_____ 8. Père-Lachaise	H.	un quartier moderne avec un musée et un théâtre
_____ 9. Notre-Dame	I.	le musée où l'on peut voir *la Joconde*
_____ 10. la Bastille	J.	le tombeau de Napoléon

20

Read what certain people did this past weekend. Then choose the most logical site from the list to tell where they went.

la Géode	**les Champs-Élysées**	**la tour Eiffel**
la Sainte-Chapelle	**la Défense**	**le musée d'Orsay**
le Louvre	**Montmartre**	**la Seine**

Modèle: Sandrine et sa famille ont visité la Villette pour voir un film.
Ils sont allés à la Géode.

1. Karine est allée au musée qui est près des jardins des Tuileries.

____

2. Normand et sa famille ont vu une petite église sur l'île de la Cité.

____

3. Tu es allé dans un quartier moderne.

____

4. Renée et Gilberte ont fait un tour en bateau.

____

5. Jean-Philippe a regardé Paris du Sacré-Cœur.

____

6. Élisabeth et toi, vous avez marché sur une avenue près de l'arc de triomphe.

____

7. J'ai vu "la Grande Dame de Paris."

____

8. Alain et moi, nous avons vu des tableaux de Renoir et de Monet.

____

POUR TOI

Superlative of adjectives

To describe someone or something as having the most of a certain quality as compared to all others, use the superlative construction:

le/la/les + **plus** + adjective

Both the definite article and the adjective agree in gender and in number with the noun.

Ces quartiers sont **les plus modernes**.

If an adjective usually precedes a noun, its superlative form also precedes it. If an adjective usually follows a noun, so does its superlative form.

Paris est **la plus belle** ville.

Le français est le cours **le plus intéressant**.

21 Write a sentence using the superlative construction.

Modèles: une ville (grand)
C'est la plus grande ville.

une ville (cosmopolite)
C'est la ville la plus cosmopolite.

1. une affiche (beau) ____
2. une voiture (joli) ____
3. une jupe (court) ____
4. un musée (petit) ____

5. un ordinateur (cher) ______________________________
6. une femme (généreux) ______________________________
7. un élève (intelligent) ______________________________
8. un homme (vieux) ______________________________

22

Elementary school children often exaggerate when they talk about their families and the various things they have. Complete the sentences begun by some young French children playing in the Luxembourg Gardens.

Modèle: (voiture/beau) Mon frère a....
Mon frère a la plus belle voiture du monde!

1. (bateau/grand) Mon père a....
____
2. (femme/généreux) Ma grand-mère est....
____
3. (vélo/joli) J'ai....
____
4. (voiture/formidable) Nous avons acheté....
____
5. (grand-père/sympa) Et moi, j'ai....
____
6. (tableau/cher) Mon oncle a acheté....
____
7. (jeux vidéo/intéressant) Ma sœur et moi, nous avons....
____
8. (dentiste/diligent) Ma mère est....
____

23 Imagine that your French pen pal asks you some questions about people and things in the United States. Answer these questions using the superlative construction.

Modèle: Qui est le joueur de basket le plus riche?
Michael Jordan est le joueur de basket le plus riche.

1. Quelle est la plus grande ville?

   ____

2. Quel est le plus bel état (*state*)?

   ____

3. Quelle est l'université la plus célèbre?

   ____

4. Qui est le président le plus intelligent?

   ____

5. Quelle est l'émission (*program*) de télé la plus intéressante?

   ____

6. Quel est le film le plus amusant?

   ____

7. Quel est le groupe de rock le plus populaire?

   ____

8. Quelle est la voiture la plus chère?

   ____

24 Describe your city or town by answering the following questions.

Modèle: Quel est le plus grand bâtiment (*building*) de ta ville?
La banque est le plus grand bâtiment de ma ville.

1. Quel est le plus beau quartier de ta ville?

   ____

2. Quel est le plus vieux quartier de ta ville?

   ____

3. Quel est le plus joli parc de ta ville?

   ____

4. Quelle est la rue la plus longue de ta ville?

____

5. Quelle est la plus grande école de ta ville?

____

6. Quel est le musée le plus important de ta ville?

____

7. Quel est le magasin le plus chic de ta ville?

____

8. Quel est le restaurant le plus cher de ta ville?

____

25 Tell what sights of Paris you would like to visit and why you would like to see them. Use the superlative construction to describe each one. Mention at least six different places in Paris in your paragraph.

Modèle: *Je voudrais visiter le Louvre pour voir* la Joconde. La Joconde *est le tableau le plus célèbre du monde.*

____

____

____

____

____

____

____

____

____

____

____

____

Answers

Unité 1

Leçon A

1 Answers will vary. (Example: FaBrice)

2 Answers will vary. (Example: PoitraS)

3

P	D	A	V	I	D	A	S	N
G	U	L	N	H	E	L	A	S
A	O	A	D	J	A	D	N	I
Y	M	I	U	A	I	S	A	K
J	H	N	K	A	R	I	N	E
S	A	I	N	O	S	A	D	N
Y	M	É	R	É	J	N	R	S
C	H	J	A	M	D	A	É	I

Boys: Alain, André, David, Jérémy, Mahmoud

Girls: Adja, Karine, Nadia, Saleh, Sonia

4
1. Bonjour, Mademoiselle.
2. Bonjour, Madame.
3. Bonjour, Madame.
4. Bonjour, Monsieur.
5. Bonjour, Mademoiselle.
6. Bonjour, Monsieur.
7. Bonjour, Madame.
8. Bonjour, Mademoiselle.

5
1. Salut/Bonjour
2. Bonjour
3. Bonjour
4. Salut/Bonjour
5. Bonjour
6. Bonjour
7. Salut/Bonjour
8. Salut/Bonjour

6 Tu, Je, te, t', m'

7 i,s,é,e
P,d,u,p,p,l,l,s,o,e,n,t
m,e,l,l
a,u
o,n,o,o,n,i,u,r

Leçon B

8
1. six, huit, dix
2. trois, deux, un
3. cinq, sept, neuf
4. seize, dix-huit, vingt
5. quinze, dix-sept, dix-neuf
6. douze, seize, vingt
7. quatorze, treize, douze
8. douze, onze, dix

9
1. douze, quatorze
2. sept, neuf
3. deux, quatre
4. dix-sept, dix-neuf
5. onze, treize
6. six, huit
7. treize, quinze
8. dix-huit, vingt
9. seize, dix-huit
10. un, trois

10
1. sept
2. seize
3. deux
4. vingt
5. quatorze
6. huit
7. quinze
8. trois

11 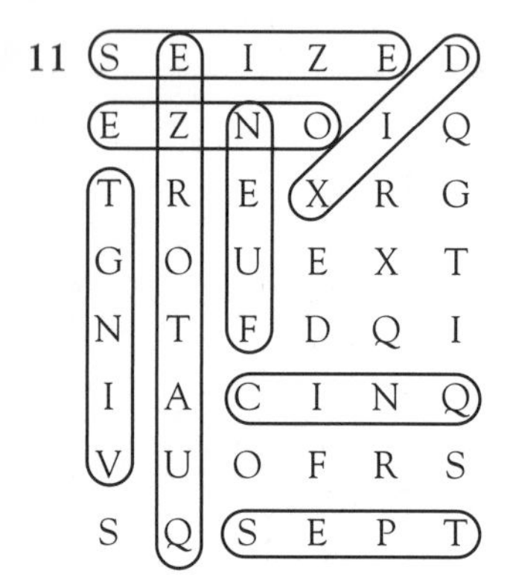

12 1. onze
2. quatorze
3. douze
4. treize
5. seize
6. quinze
7. dix-neuf
8. vingt

13 1. cinq
2. trois
3. sept
4. dix-sept
5. quatre
6. dix-huit
7. neuf
8. six

14 1. huit
2. douze
3. dix
4. dix-huit
5. vingt
6. deux
7. seize
8. neuf

15 Salut/Bonjour
je te présente
Bonjour
Bonjour
Salut/Bonjour
Bonjour/Salut! Tu t'appelles comment?
Bonjour/Salut! Je m'appelle
Bonjour/Salut

Unité 2

Leçon A

1 1. D/F; v/n, s
2. D/F; v/n, s
3. C; j
4. G; l
5. I; n
6. H; l, l
7. E; t
8. A; l, s
9. B; l, l, s

2 1. Charles
2. Myriam et Yasmine
3. Luc et Sylvie
4. Denise
5. Luc et Sylvie
6. Charles
7. Denise
8. Myriam et Yasmine

3 1. vous
2. tu
3. vous
4. vous
5. vous
6. tu
7. vous
8. tu

4 1. vous
2. tu
3. vous
4. vous
5. vous
6. vous
7. tu
8. vous

5 1. e, a, e
2. o, u, e
3. é, o, u, e
4. é, é, o, e
5. i, e
6. a, i, e
7. a, e
8. é, u, i, e

6

7 1. regarder
2. aller
3. écouter
4. jouer
5. jouer
6. étudier
7. skier
8. nager

8 Answers will vary.

9 Answers will vary.

10 1. tu
2. vous
3. elles
4. Elle
5. Nous
6. J
7. Ils
8. Il

11 1. e
2. ent
3. e
4. ons
5. e
6. ent
7. ez
8. es

12 1. skie
2. nagez
3. jouent
4. étudions
5. aiment
6. joue
7. écoutent
8. regarde

13

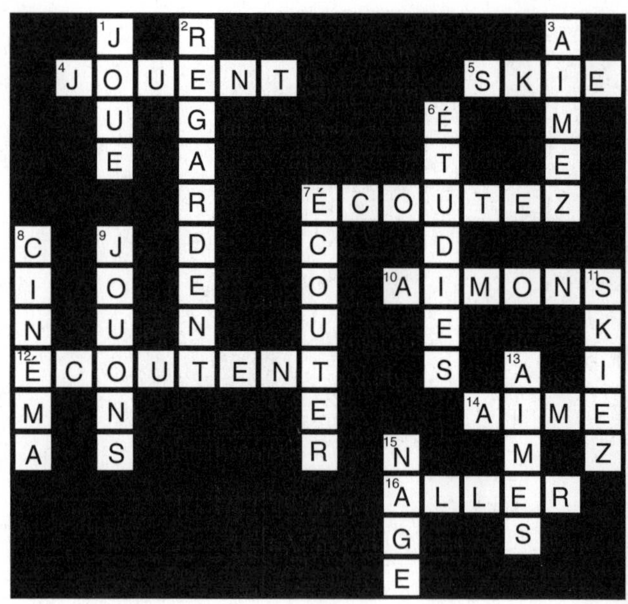

Leçon B

14 Answers will vary.

15 Answers will vary.

16 Answers will vary.

17 Answers will vary.

18 Answers will vary.

19 Answers will vary.

Leçon C

20 Answers will vary.

21

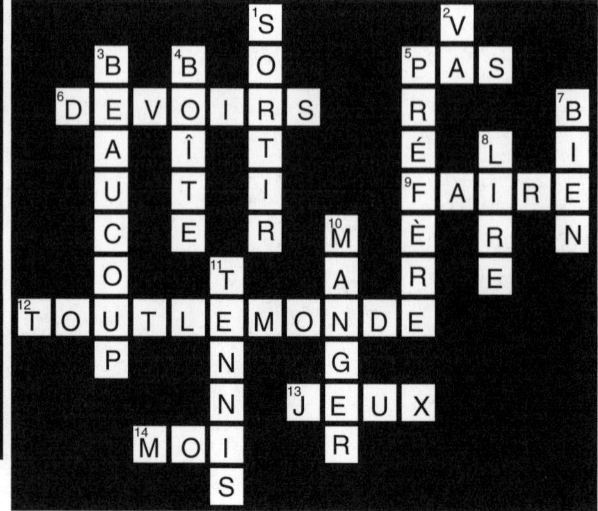

22
1. Sandrine n'aime pas faire les devoirs.
2. Michel et Louis n'aiment pas faire du shopping.
3. Chloé n'aime pas jouer au volley.
4. Édouard et Caroline n'aiment pas danser.
5. Céline n'aime pas sortir.
6. Aïcha n'aime pas dormir.
7. Abdel-Cader n'aime pas jouer aux jeux vidéo.
8. Margarette et Latifa n'aiment pas manger de la pizza.

23
1. Nous ne jouons pas au volley.
2. Diane regarde la télé.
3. Amine écoute la techno.
4. Renée et Ariane ne dansent pas bien.
5. Vous skiez dans les Alpes.
6. M. et Mme Dumont n'arrivent pas le dix.
7. Tu n'étudies pas pour l'interro.
8. Je n'aime pas beaucoup les sports.

24 Answers will vary.

Unité 3

Leçon A

1 Possible answers:

1. J'ai faim.
2. Très bien.
3. Comme ci, comme ça.
4. J'ai soif.
5. Très mal.
6. Très bien.
7. J'ai faim.
8. Très bien.

2
1. e, a, i
2. o, u, a, o
3. i, o
4. u, a
5. e, e, a
6. o, u, a, e
7. i, a
8. e, e, o

3 1. D 2. A 3. F 4. B 5. C 6. E 7. D 8. F

4
1. vont
2. vais
3. allons
4. vas
5. vont
6. allez
7. allez

5

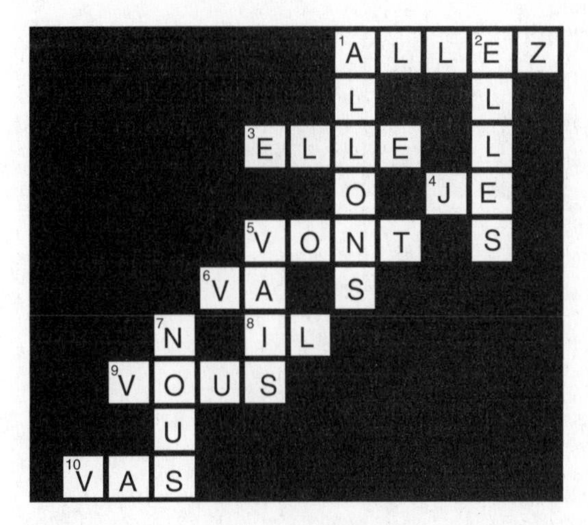

6
4 — Il est quatre heures.
5 — Il est cinq heures.
6 — Il est six heures.
7 — Il est sept heures.
8 — Il est huit heures.
9 — Il est neuf heures.
10 — Il est dix heures.
11 — Il est onze heures.

7
1. 6h00
2. 1h00
3. 9h00
4. 11h00
5. 7h00
6. 10h00
7. 3h00
8. 5h00

8
1. Il est dix heures.
2. Il est midi.
3. Il est deux heures.
4. Il est trois heures.
5. Il est onze heures.
6. Il est cinq heures.
7. Il est neuf heures.
8. Il est huit heures.

Leçon B

9
1. vanille
2. pomme
3. jambon
4. frites
5. raisins
6. orange
7. fromage
8. chocolat

10 Boissons: limonade, jus de pomme, jus d'orange, coca, café, jus de raisin, eau minérale

Sandwichs: hot-dog, hamburger, sandwich au fromage, sandwich au jambon

Desserts: glace à la vanille, glace au chocolat, crêpe

11

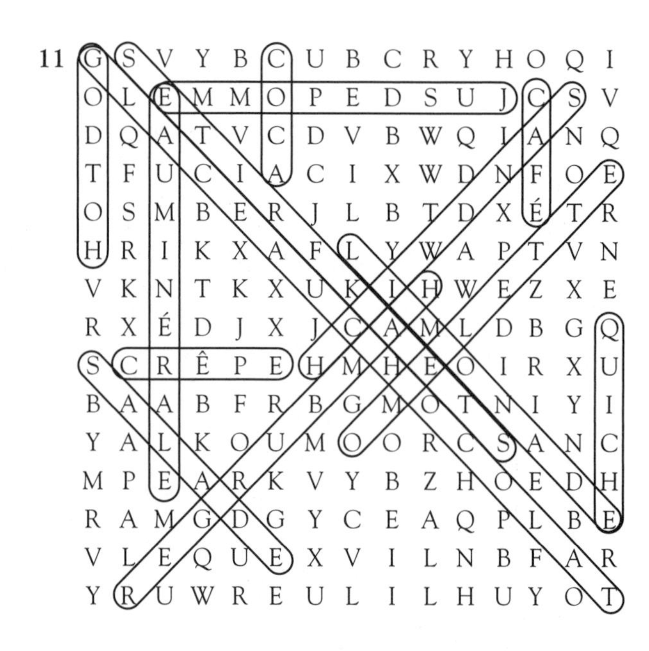

12 J'ai faim: un steak-frites, une glace, une salade, une quiche, un hot-dog, un sandwich au jambon, une omelette, une crêpe

J'ai soif: un coca, une eau minérale, un jus de raisin, un café, un jus d'orange, une limonade

13 Answers will vary.

Leçon C

14 Possible answers:
1. one 200-euro bill, one 50-euro bill and one 10-euro bill
2. one 500-euro bill, one 100-euro bill and one 50-euro bill
3. one 50-euro bill and two 20-euro bills
4. one 100-euro bill, one 50-euro bill, one 20-euro bill and one 10-euro bill
5. one 20-euro bill and one 10-euro bill
6. one 100-euro bill, one 20-euro bill, one 10-euro bill and one 5-euro bill
7. one 50-euro bill, one 20-euro bill, one 10-euro bill and one 5-euro bill
8. two 200-euro bills, one 50-euro bill, one 20-euro bill and one 10-euro bill

15 1. D 2. E 3. G 4. A 5. B 6. F 7. C

16
1. vingt et un
2. soixante-douze
3. quatre-vingt-six
4. cinquante-quatre
5. cent
6. trente-sept
7. quatre-vingt-treize
8. soixante-cinq
9. quarante-huit

17
1. quatre-vingts
2. quatre-vingt-quatre
3. quatre-vingt-seize
4. soixante-trois
5. soixante-douze
6. quatre-vingt-un
7. quatre-vingt-dix
8. soixante-dix-huit

18

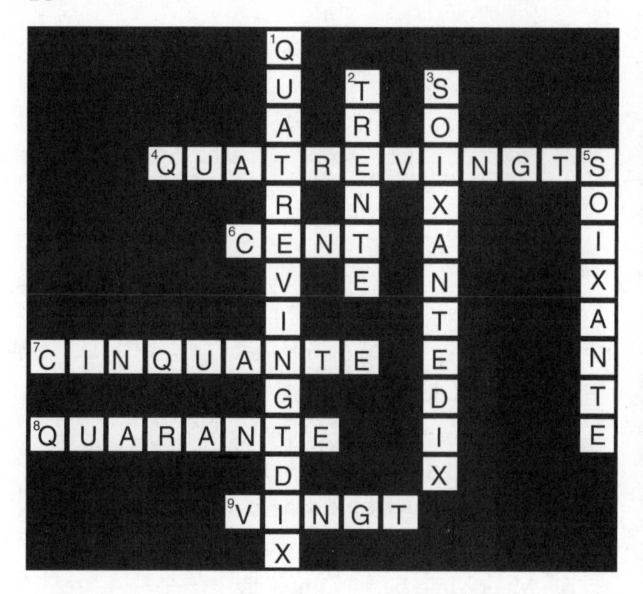

19 The circled numbers are vingt-neuf, trente-trois, soixante-seize, soixante-douze, soixante-dix-huit, trente-neuf, quatre-vingt-huit, vingt-quatre, soixante-cinq and quarante-six.

The last card is a winner.

20
1. cinquante-sept, cinquante-neuf
2. trente et un, trente-trois
3. soixante-quatorze, soixante-seize
4. quatre-vingt-dix-huit, cent
5. soixante et un, soixante-trois
6. quatre-vingt-un, quatre-vingt-trois
7. vingt-cinq, vingt-sept
8. quatre-vingt-neuf, quatre-vingt-onze

21
B: douze, quatre, huit, treize, onze
I: vingt-deux, dix-neuf, seize, vingt-six, vingt-huit
N: quarante et un, trente-neuf, trente-quatre, trente-deux, quarante-cinq
G: quarante-sept, quarante-six, cinquante-huit, quarante-trois, cinquante et un
O: soixante et onze, soixante-quinze, soixante-deux, soixante-dix, soixante-six

22

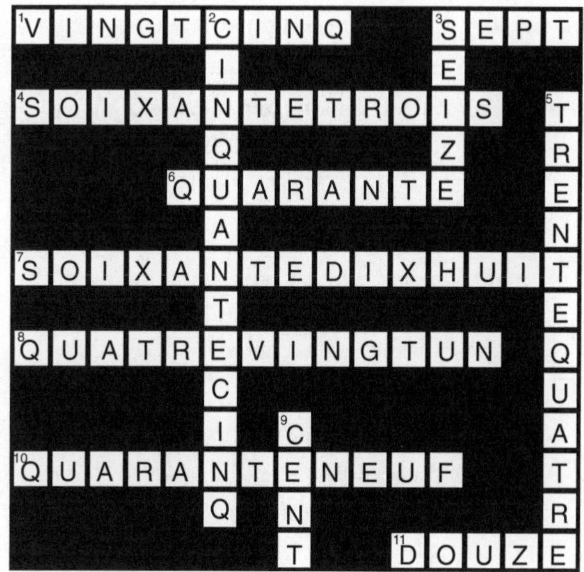

23
1. Le, Il
2. La, Elle
3. L', Elle
4. Le, Il
5. La, Elle
6. Le, Il
7. Le, Il
8. L', Elle

24
1. Le sandwich au jambon coûte quatre euros quarante-deux.
2. Le thé coûte trois euros cinq.
3. La glace au chocolat coûte cinq euros dix-huit.
4. La crêpe coûte quatre euros cinquante-sept.
5. Le sandwich au fromage coûte quatre euros vingt-sept.
6. La limonade coûte trois euros vingt.
7. Le steak-frites coûte dix euros vingt et un.
8. La glace à la vanille coûte quatre euros quatre-vingt-huit.

25
1. les, Ils
2. des, ils
3. les, des, Elles
4. des, elles
5. les, Elles

Unité 4

Leçon A

1 Possible answers:

sur un bureau: un dictionnaire, un CD, une cassette, un ordinateur, une disquette, une vidéocassette

sur une table d'étudiant: un sac à dos, une feuille de papier

dans un sac à dos: un crayon, une trousse, un cahier, un livre, un stylo

2 Answers will vary.

3 Answers will vary.

4 1. D 2. A 3. E 4. C 5. B 6. F 7. D 8. C

5

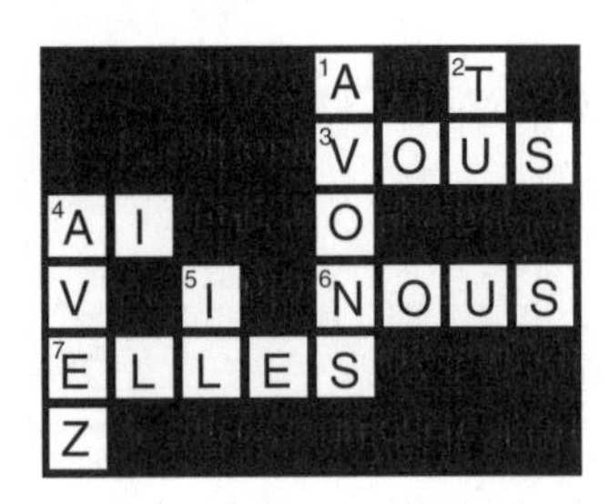

6 1. Oui, le professeur a un ordinateur dans la salle de classe.
2. Oui, les élèves ont des livres dans leurs sacs à dos.
3. J'ai des crayons/stylos.
4. La salle de classe a... fenêtres.
5. Oui, le professeur a des vidéocassettes pour le magnétoscope.
6. Oui, nous avons une pendule dans la salle de classe.
7. Oui, les élèves ont les devoirs dans leurs cahiers.
8. Oui, j'ai un sac à dos.

7 1. faim
2. besoin
3. faim
4. besoin
5. soif
6. besoin
7. soif
8. faim

8 1. Vous avez besoin d'un livre.
2. Le sac à dos est avec le dictionnaire./Le dictionnaire est avec le sac à dos.
3. Le tableau est derrière la prof.
4. La vidéocassette est dans le magnétoscope.
5. L'ordinateur est sur le bureau.
6. M. et Mme Bernier ont soif.
7. Le taille-crayon est dans la salle de classe.
8. J'ai une feuille de papier.

Leçon B

9 1. samedi
2. mercredi
3. jeudi
4. dimanche
5. mardi
6. vendredi
7. lundi

10 1. D 2. G 3. B 4. F 5. C 6. A 7. E

11

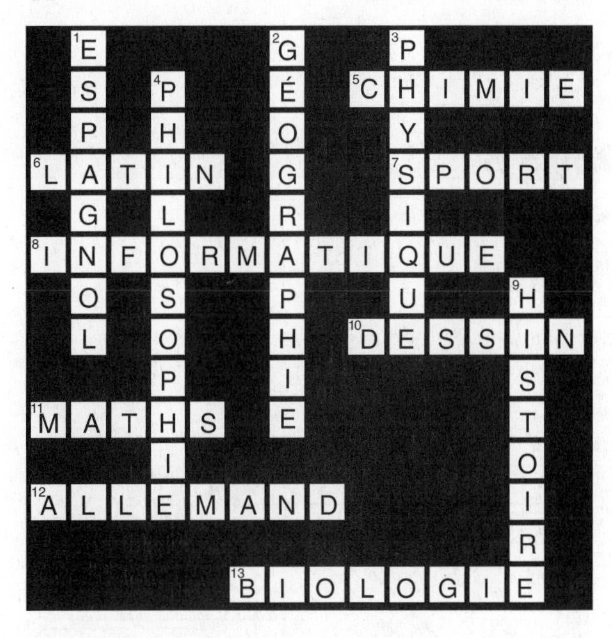

12 les arts: le dessin, la musique

les langues: l'anglais, l'allemand, l'espagnol, le français, le latin

les sciences: la biologie, la physique, la chimie

les sciences sociales: la philosophie, l'histoire, la géographie

13
1. u, i, i
2. i, i, i, e
3. e, i, i
4. o, u, i, i, o
5. e, e, i, i, e
6. o, i, i
7. o, u, i, i, e
8. e, e, i, i

14
1. finit
2. finissent
3. finissez
4. finis
5. finissent
6. finis
7. finit
8. finissons

15

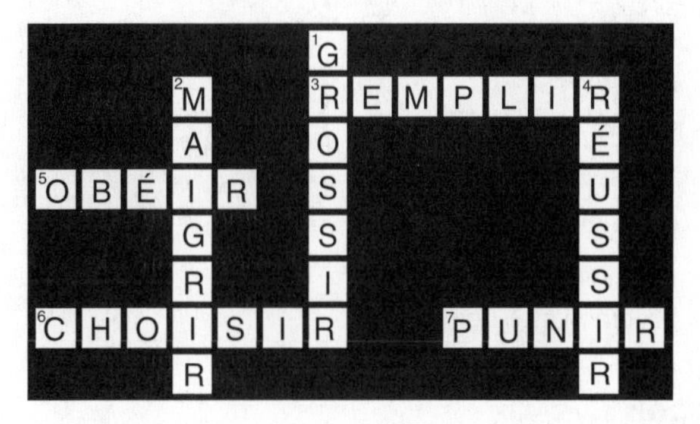

16
1. choisissons
2. choisissent
3. choisis
4. choisissez
5. choisissent
6. choisit
7. choisit
8. choisis

17
1. Nous
2. Il
3. je/tu
4. vous
5. elles
6. Il/Elle/On
7. Vous
8. Je/Tu

18
1. punit
2. obéissons
3. maigrissent
4. remplis
5. grossissent
6. réussit
7. finis
8. choisissez

19 1. cinq
2. vingt
3. quinze
4. dix
5. vingt-cinq
6. quarante
7. cinquante-trois
8. cinquante-huit

Leçon C

20 1. Il est seize heures.
2. Il est vingt heures.
3. Il est treize heures.
4. Il est quinze heures.
5. Il est vingt et une heures.
6. Il est onze heures.
7. Il est une heure.
8. Il est midi.

21 1. D 2. G 3. E 4. B 5. H 6. C 7. A 8. F

22 1. Il est une heure moins le quart.
2. Il est midi et demi.
3. Il est cinq heures et quart.
4. Il est cinq heures cinq.
5. Il est neuf heures trente.
6. Il est minuit moins vingt.
7. Il est six heures vingt-cinq.
8. Il est sept heures et quart.

23 1. Non, il est huit heures et quart./Non, il est huit heures quinze.
2. Non, il est neuf heures et demie./Non, il est neuf heures trente.
3. Non, il est sept heures moins le quart./Non, il est six heures quarante-cinq.
4. Non, il est trois heures vingt-cinq.
5. Non, il est sept heures trente-cinq./Non, il est huit heures moins vingt-cinq.
6. Oui, il est onze heures dix.
7. Oui, il est cinq heures et quart.
8. Non, il est cinq heures moins cinq./Non, il est quatre heures cinquante-cinq.

24 Answers will vary.

25 Answers will vary.

Unité 5

Leçon A

1 1. A 2. E 3. C 4. F 5. B 6. H 7. D 8. G

2 ai, noirs/roux/blonds, yeux, ont, cheveux, ans, noirs/roux/blonds, a, noirs/roux/blonds, âge

3
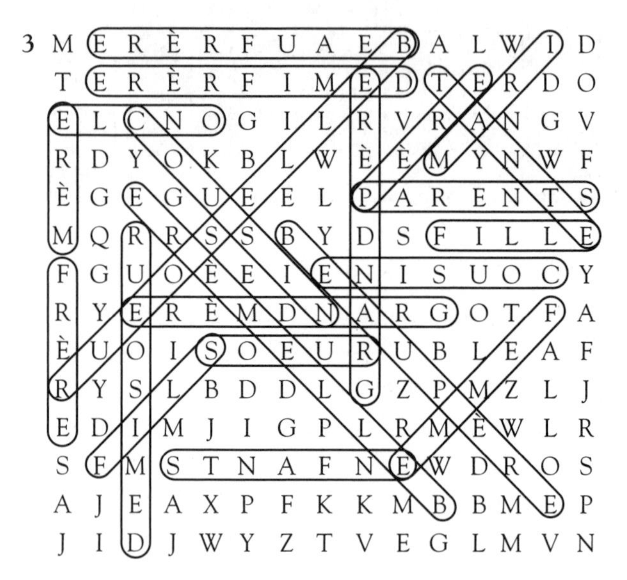

Male: un beau-frère, un beau-père, un cousin, un demi-frère, des enfants, un fils, un frère, un grand-mère, un mari, un oncle, des parents, un père

Female: une belle-mère, une belle-sœur, une cousine, une demi-sœur, des enfants, une femme, une fille, une grand-mère, une mère, une sœur, une tante

4 Answers will vary.

5 1. D/F 2. G 3. D/F 4. B 5. C 6. A/H 7. E 8. A/H

6 1. mes, mon
2. ses, son
3. leurs, leurs
4. nos, notre
5. tes, ton
6. son, sa
7. votre, vos
8. son, sa

7 1. quel, ans
2. a, Elle
3. âge, a
4. quel, ans
5. ont, Elles
6. as, ai, Answers will vary.

8 1. Ton oncle a quel âge?
2. Ta belle-sœur a quel âge?
3. Ton beau-frère a quel âge?
4. Tes parents ont quel âge?
5. Ta grand-mère a quel âge?
6. Ton grand-père a quel âge?
7. Ton cousin a quel âge?
8. Ta cousine a quel âge?

Leçon B

9 1. février
2. juin
3. décembre
4. octobre
5. mars
6. juillet
7. avril
8. novembre
9. août
10. janvier
11. mai
12. septembre

10 1. F 2. K 3. A 4. I 5. E 6. B 7. H 8. C 9. J 10. L 11. D 12. G

11 1. mille neuf cent quinze euros
2. deux mille quatre cent dix euros
3. cinq mille huit cent soixante euros
4. deux mille six cent vingt euros
5. mille deux cent cinquante euros
6. quatre mille trois cent cinq euros
7. trois mille deux cent quarante-cinq euros
8. quatre mille trois cent soixante-quinze euros

12 1. D 2. G 3. A 4. H 5. B 6. E 7. F 8. C

13 1. Thierry a un chien.
2. Sonia a un cheval.
3. Fabienne a cinq poissons rouges.
4. Sabrina a un oiseau.
5. Hervé a quatre chiens.
6. Olivier a un chat.
7. Jeanne a un poisson rouge.
8. Gilberte a trois chats.

14 1. C 2. A 3. B 4. H 5. F 6. G 7. D 8. E

15

16 1. suis
2. sont
3. es
4. sommes
5. sont
6. est
7. est
8. êtes

17 a, son, est, Sa, ses, ont, sont, Leur, leurs

18 1. le huit janvier
2. le vingt mars
3. le onze novembre
4. le quatorze juillet
5. le trente octobre
6. le premier mai
7. le cinq juin
8. le trente et un décembre

19 Answers will vary.

Leçon C

20 1. G 2. H 3. J 4. F 5. C 6. K 7. D 8. A 9. B 10. E 11. I

21 1. F 2. E 3. G 4. A 5. H 6. B 7. D 8. C

22

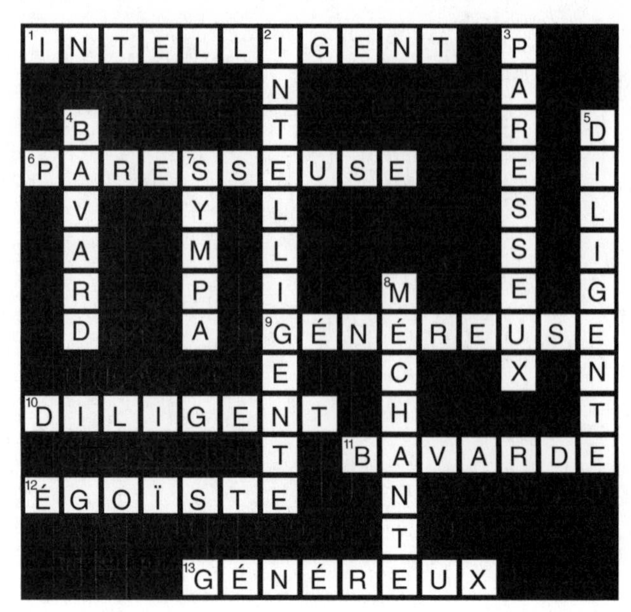

23 1. timide
2. intelligent(e)s
3. bête
4. belle
5. bavardes
6. beaux
7. diligente
8. généreuse

24 1. Sa sœur est méchante.
2. Sa grand-mère n'est pas timide.
3. Son oncle n'est pas beau.
4. Ses cousines sont bêtes.
5. Sa prof de chimie n'est pas paresseuse.
6. Ses grands-parents sont généreux.

25 Answers will vary.

Unité 6

Leçon A

1
1. Il est allemand.
2. Elle est mexicaine.
3. Ils sont français.
4. Il est chinois.
5. Ils sont anglais.
6. Il est canadien.
7. Ils sont américains.
8. Il est espagnol.
9. Elles sont japonaises.

2
1. Elle est française.
2. Elle est espagnole.
3. Il est japonais.
4. Ils sont canadiens.
5. Il est mexicain.
6. Elle est chinoise.
7. Ils sont italiens.
8. Elle est anglaise.
9. Ils sont vietnamiens.

3

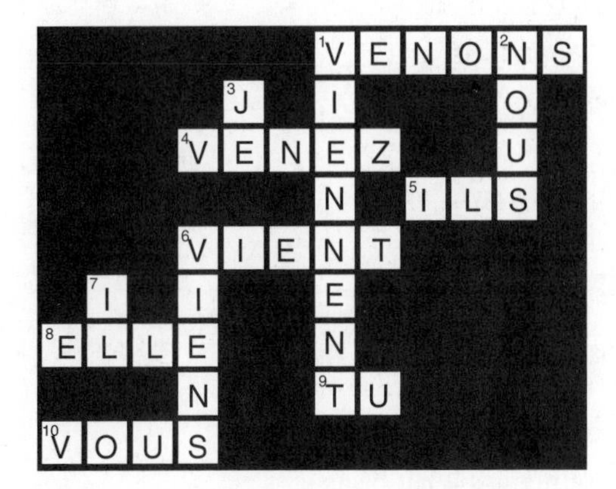

4
1. Elle revient du Japon.
2. Nous revenons d'Allemagne.
3. Tu reviens du Mexique.
4. Elles reviennent d'Espagne.
5. Il revient du Canada.
6. Je reviens de Chine.
7. Vous revenez de France.
8. Ils reviennent d'Italie.

5
1. C'est le stylo de l'élève qui étudie l'espagnol.
2. C'est le sac à dos de la fille avec les yeux bleus.
3. Ce sont les crayons des garçons qui jouent au basket.
4. C'est le CD de la sœur de Bertrand.
5. C'est le livre de français de l'étudiant qui n'étudie pas.
6. C'est la trousse du frère de Bruno.
7. C'est le dictionnaire de la cousine de Yasmine.
8. Ce sont les vidéocassettes des professeurs.

6
3. D'où reviens-tu?/Je reviens d'Angleterre.
4. D'où revenez-vous?/Je reviens du Japon.
5. D'où reviens-tu?/Je reviens d'Espagne.
6. D'où revenez-vous?/Je reviens du Vietnam.
7. D'où revenez-vous?/Nous revenons d'Allemagne.
8. D'où revenez-vous?/Nous revenons d'Italie.
9. D'où reviens-tu?/Je reviens du Mexique.
10. D'où revenez-vous?/Je reviens des États-Unis.

7
1. Est-ce que tu es canadienne?
2. Est-ce que tu es espagnole?
3. Est-ce que tu es mexicain?
4. Est-ce que tu es chinois?
5. Est-ce que tu es japonaise?
6. Est-ce que tu es française?
7. Est-ce que tu es allemand?
8. Est-ce que tu es italienne?

8 1. D 2. G 3. A 4. F 5. B 6. H 7. C 8. E

9
1. Comment est-ce que tu t'appelles?
2. Pourquoi est-ce que tu es aux États-Unis?
3. D'où est-ce que tu viens?
4. Est-ce que tu es français?
5. Qui sont les membres de ta famille?
6. Tu ressembles à ton père?
7. Où est-ce que tu vas à l'école?
8. Avec qui est-ce que tu vas au cinéma?

Leçon B

10

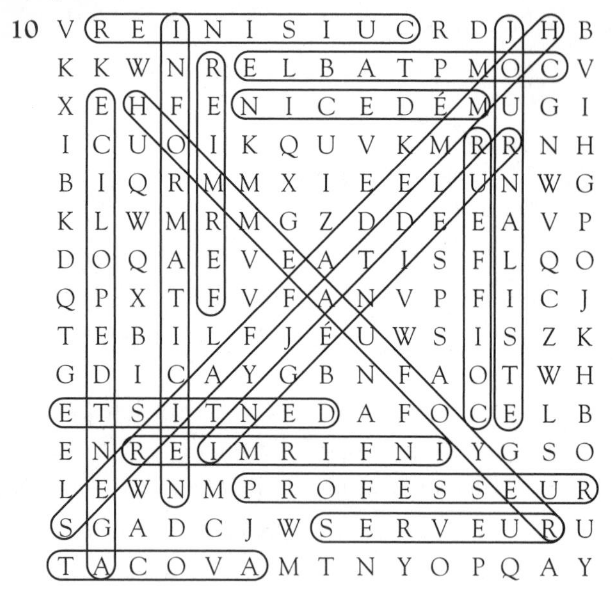

11 Possible answers:

1. Est-ce qu'il est homme d'affaires ou informaticien?
2. Est-ce qu'elle est journaliste ou femme d'affaires?
3. Est-ce qu'elle est cuisinière ou serveuse?
4. Est-ce qu'il est agent de police ou avocat?
5. Est-ce qu'il est dentiste ou médecin?
6. Est-ce qu'elle est professeur ou cuisinière?
7. Est-ce qu'elle est comptable ou informaticienne?

12
1. Ils n'ont pas de dictionnaire.
2. Elle n'a pas de trousse.
3. Il n'a pas de sac à dos.
4. Ils n'ont pas de stylos.
5. Elle n'a pas de livre de français.
6. Ils n'ont pas de feuilles de papier.
7. Il n'a pas de cassette.
8. Ils n'ont pas de disquette.

13 Answers will vary.

14
1. Quel magnétoscope?
2. Quelles cassettes françaises?
3. Quels CDs?
4. Quels stylos noirs?
5. Quel calendrier?
6. Quelle disquette?
7. Quel cahier gris?
8. Quelles vidéocassettes?

15
1. Quels jours est-ce que vous travaillez?
2. Quelles heures est-ce que vous travaillez?
3. Quel ordinateur est-ce que vous avez?
4. Quels chats sont méchants?
5. Quels chiens sont intelligents?
6. Quel oiseau est sympa?
7. Quel cheval est-ce que vous préférez?
8. Quelle musique est-ce que vous aimez?

16
1. C'est, Elle est
2. Elle est, elle est
3. C'est, Il est
4. Ils sont, Ce sont
5. Ce sont, Ils sont
6. Il est, C'est, il est
7. Elles sont, Ce sont
8. Elles sont, elles sont

17 Answers will vary.

Leçon C

18
1. En hiver il fait froid.
2. En automne il pleut.
3. En été il fait du soleil.
4. Au printemps il fait beau.
5. En hiver il neige.
6. En été il fait chaud.
7. En automne il fait frais.
8. Au printemps il fait du vent.

19 Answers will vary.

20

21
1. fait
2. faisons
3. font
4. fais
5. fait
6. faisons
7. font
8. faites

22 Answers will vary.

23
1. Tes amis parlent-ils anglais?
2. Tes amis et toi regardez-vous la télé après les cours?
3. Tes amis aiment-ils aller au cinéma?
4. Tes parents travaillent-ils beaucoup?
5. Ton père est-il ingénieur?
6. Ta famille et toi faites-vous du vélo?
7. Ton frère va-t-il souvent au fast-food?
8. Ta sœur nage-t-elle?

24 Possible answers:
1. Quel âge as-tu?
2. À quelle heure arrives-tu à l'école?
3. Aimes-tu tes professeurs?
4. Quel cours préfères-tu?
5. Où mangez-vous à midi?
6. À quelle heure regardes-tu la télé?
7. À qui téléphones-tu?
8. Quand fais-tu du shopping?

Unité 7

Leçon A

1
1. un pantalon
2. un magasin
3. un anorak
4. un blouson
5. une boutique
6. un ensemble
7. un costume
8. un maillot
9. une chemise
10. un chapeau

2

3 Answers will vary.

4 Answers will vary.

5 Possible answers:
1. Tu vas faire du vélo.
2. Nous allons étudier/faire les devoirs.
3. Je vais manger.
4. Elle va skier.
5. Ils vont faire du shopping.
6. Vous allez écouter de la musique.
7. Il va nager.
8. Elles vont regarder un film.

6
1. Il va faire du footing.
2. Nous allons jouer au basket.
3. Tu vas faire du sport.
4. Elle va sortir.
5. Vous allez jouer au volley.
6. Ils vont faire un tour.
7. Je vais faire du roller.
8. Elles vont jouer au foot.

7
1. Vous étudiez. Vous n'allez pas jouer aux jeux vidéo.
2. Il étudie. Il ne va pas faire du vélo.
3. Tu étudies. Tu ne vas pas écouter la radio.
4. Ils étudient. Ils ne vont pas regarder la télé.
5. Nous étudions. Nous n'allons pas faire du footing.
6. Elles étudient. Elles ne vont pas aller au cinéma.
7. Elle étudie. Elle ne va pas faire du shopping.
8. J'étudie. Je ne vais pas aller au fast-food.

8 Answers will vary.

9
1. au
2. au
3. à la
4. aux
5. à l'
6. aux

10 Possible answers:
1. au grand magasin
2. au centre commercial
3. à la boum
4. à l'école
5. au café
6. au magasin
7. au fast-food
8. à la cantine

Leçon B

11
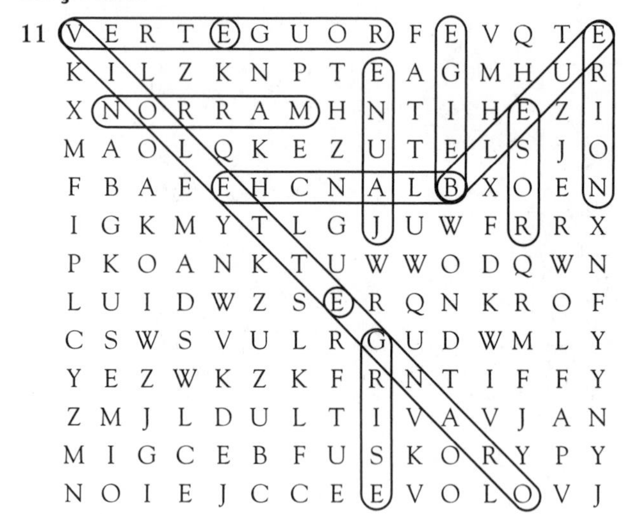

12 1. G 2. C 3. A 4. E 5. H 6. B 7. D 8. F

13
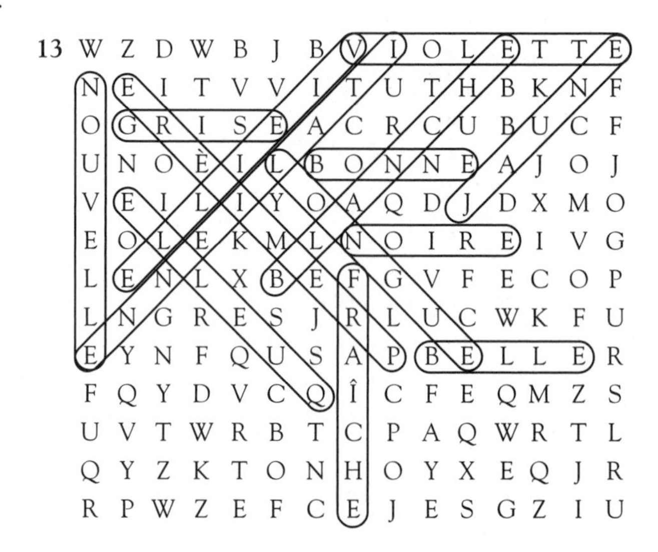

14
1. gris
2. rouge
3. bon
4. mauvaise
5. fraîche
6. vietnamienne
7. première
8. moche
9. grande
10. blanche
11. espagnole
12. courte
13. orange
14. bel
15. allemande

15
1. Marc et Céline ont deux petits vélos.
2. M. Djibouti adore la musique américaine.
3. On passe un bon film au Gaumont.
4. Notre professeur de sciences porte un vieux costume.
5. Donnez-moi une boisson fraîche, s'il vous plaît.
6. Je voudrais une glace italienne.
7. Oh là là! C'est une grande boutique!
8. Paul va acheter un jean noir.

16
1. Mes cousines ont deux jolis desserts.
2. Mon père a deux petites crêpes.
3. Ma sœur a un bon steak-frites.
4. Ma mère a un jus d'orange frais.
5. Mon oncle a une belle tarte aux pommes.
6. Ma grand-mère a un sandwich chaud.
7. Mon grand-père a une omelette espagnole.
8. J'ai une grande glace au chocolat.

17 Answers will vary.

18
1. achète
2. achetons
3. achète
4. achètent
5. achètes
6. achète
7. achetez

19
1. préférons
2. préfèrent
3. préfère
4. préfèrent
5. préférez
6. préfères
7. préfère

Leçon C

20
1. En France, il fait du quarante.
2. En France, elle fait du quarante-deux.
3. En France, il fait du quarante.
4. En France, elle fait du deux.
5. En France, elle fait du quarante.
6. En France, il fait du quarante-huit.
7. En France, il fait du trente-six.
8. En France, il fait du quarante-quatre.

21 acheter, centre, viens, taille, fais, vais, vendeur, combien

22
1. vend
2. vendent
3. vendez
4. vendons
5. vendent
6. vends
7. vend
8. vends

23
1. attendent
2. attend
3. attendent
4. attendons
5. attends
6. attend
7. attends
8. attendez

24
1. répond
2. descends
3. attends
4. entendent
5. rendez
6. perdons
7. vend

25

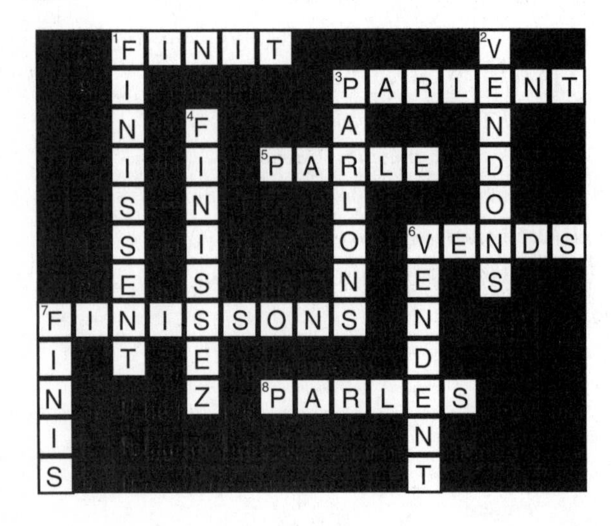

Unité 8

Leçon A

1

P	O	M	M	E	D	E	T	E	R	R	E	W	U	K
Q	R	Z	D	T	Q	C	R	E	V	E	T	T	E	F
K	A	L	E	T	P	Z	E	M	U	G	É	L	F	S
C	N	M	J	O	C	E	V	A	I	Z	K	W	B	S
Z	G	R	H	R	Q	R	T	Y	T	O	K	J	J	K
N	E	R	A	A	Y	B	O	I	F	N	S	Z	O	N
B	T	B	E	C	M	A	C	F	T	H	A	M	I	I
N	E	A	N	O	S	S	I	O	P	S	Y	P	O	H
Z	T	K	L	T	Q	I	R	C	T	A	P	Y	O	Q
N	O	N	G	I	P	M	A	H	C	I	N	O	E	E
C	M	B	I	U	V	W	H	A	N	O	N	G	I	O
A	A	B	M	R	S	D	H	C	W	J	E	H	E	S
U	T	R	M	F	X	A	L	I	T	R	I	Q	B	G
D	E	I	G	Q	I	D	U	B	P	B	L	D	X	Z

un poisson, un légume, un haricot vert, un oignon, un champignon, un crabe, un fruit, des petits pois, une pomme de terre, une carotte, une crevette, une tomate, une orange

2 Answers will vary.

3
1. veut
2. veulent
3. voulons
4. veut
5. veux
6. voulez
7. veulent
8. veux

4
1. veux, veux
2. voulez, voulons
3. veulent, veulent
4. Veut, veut
5. voulons, voulez
6. veulent, veulent

5
1. Il peut acheter....
2. Nous pouvons acheter....
3. Vous pouvez acheter....
4. Elles peuvent acheter....
5. Tu peux acheter....
6. Je peux acheter....
7. Ils peuvent acheter....
8. Elle peut acheter....

6 Answers will vary.

7
1. ces
2. cette
3. ce
4. Cet
5. ces
6. ces
7. Cette
8. Ce

8
1. ces
2. cette
3. ce
4. cet
5. ce
6. ces
7. Cette
8. ce

9
1. Cette eau minérale est très froide.
2. Michel veut ce sandwich au fromage.
3. Cette glace au chocolat est bonne.
4. Ils peuvent manger ces oranges aujourd'hui.
5. Ma belle-mère va acheter ces sandwichs.
6. Je voudrais manger ces pommes de terre.
7. Claire peut faire cette salade.
8. Nous voulons manger ces crevettes.

Leçon B

10
1. baguette
2. mayonnaise
3. saucisson
4. lait
5. poulet
6. porc
7. pâté
8. yaourt
9. confiture
10. gâteau

Bon appétit!

11 Possible answers:
1. le bœuf, le porc
2. le gâteau, la tarte aux fraises
3. le lait, les œufs
4. le saucisson, le pâté
5. le pain, la baguette

12
à la boucherie: du poulet
à la boulangerie: des baguettes
à la charcuterie: du jambon, du pâté
à la crémerie: du beurre, du fromage, du yaourt
à la pâtisserie: des tartes aux fraises
au supermarché: de la mayonnaise, du coca, de la moutarde, de l'eau minérale

13
1. des, du
2. de l', des
3. des, de la
4. de la, du
5. du, du, de l'
6. du, des
7. du, de la
8. du, du

14
1. de la
2. du, des
3. de la
4. des
5. les, les, les
6. du, de la
7. de l'
8. Du, de la
9. De la
10. la

15
1. Non, je ne veux pas de dessert. J'ai soif.
2. Oui, je veux bien. J'ai soif.
3. Non, je ne veux pas de steak-frites. J'ai soif.
4. Non, je ne veux pas de crêpes. J'ai soif.
5. Oui, je veux bien. J'ai soif.
6. Non, je ne veux pas de quiche. J'ai soif.
7. Oui, je veux bien. J'ai soif.
8. Non, je ne veux pas de glace. J'ai soif.

16
1. Oui, je veux du coca.
2. Oui, je veux des croissants.
3. Oui, je veux de l'omelette.
4. Non, je ne veux pas de fromage.
5. Non, je ne veux pas de yaourt.
6. Non, je ne veux pas de camembert.
7. Non, je ne veux pas de glace.
8. Oui, je veux des pommes.

17

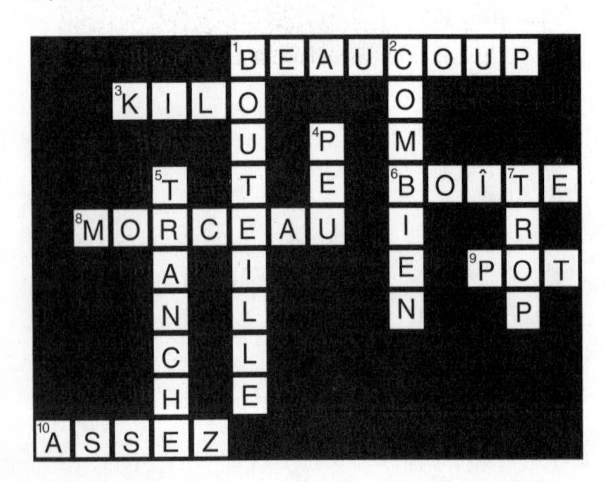

18
1. Combien d'oranges voulez-vous?
2. Combien de carottes voulez-vous?
3. Combien d'œufs voulez-vous?
4. Combien de tomates voulez-vous?
5. Combien de pommes de terre voulez-vous?
6. Combien d'oignons voulez-vous?
7. Combien de crevettes voulez-vous?
8. Combien de champignons voulez-vous?

19
1. une tranche de/un kilo de
2. un kilo de/un morceau de/une tranche de
3. un pot de
4. un kilo de/une boîte de
5. une bouteille d'
6. une bouteille de/une boîte de
7. un pot de
8. un kilo de/une tranche de
9. une bouteille de/une boîte de
10. un kilo de/une boîte de

Leçon C

20

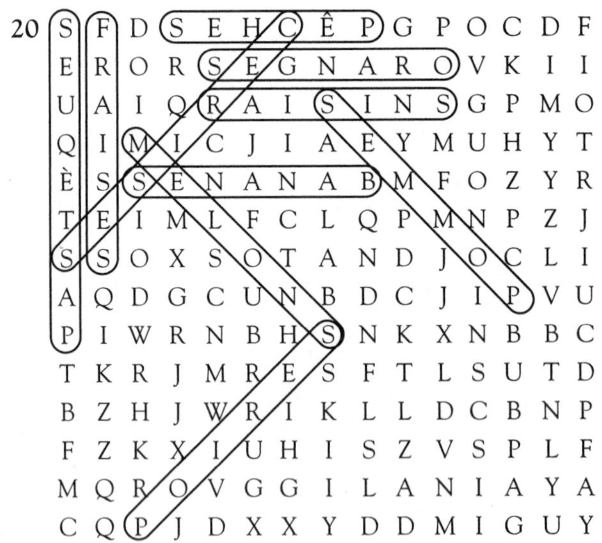

21 1. une pomme
2. une fraise, une cerise
3. une banane
4. une pastèque
5. une poire
6. un raisin
7. une orange
8. une pêche, une orange, un melon

22 1. Les raisins sont plus petits que les pommes.
2. Les pêches sont moins petites que les fraises.
3. Les oranges sont aussi petites que les pommes.
4. Les pastèques sont moins petites que les bananes.
5. Les poires sont moins petites que les cerises.
6. Les fraises sont plus petites que les pêches.
7. Les cerises sont aussi petites que les raisins.
8. Les melons sont plus petits que les pastèques.

23 1. La robe bleue est plus chère que la robe blanche.
2. Les jeans sont plus chers que les pantalons.
3. L'anorak est aussi cher que le blouson.
4. Le short vert est plus cher que le short orange.
5. Les chaussures sont moins chères que les baskets.
6. Le costume est aussi cher que le tailleur.
7. La jupe beige est plus chère que la jupe courte.
8. Le tee-shirt est moins cher que le sweat.

24 Answers will vary.

Unité 9

Leçon A

1 1. fauteuil
2. armoire
3. évier
4. lit
5. canapé
6. baignoire
7. tapis
8. placard
9. cuisinière
10. douche

2 Drawings will vary.

3

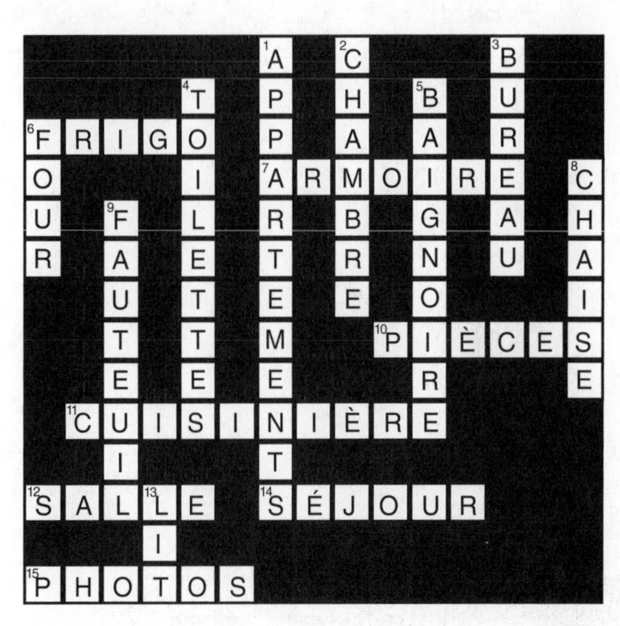

4 Answers will vary.

5 1. une
2. une
3. deux
4. deux
5. six
6. deux
7. une
8. une
9. une
10. trois

6 1. de, de
2. des, des
3. des, de
4. de, des
5. des
6. de, des, de
7. des
8. de

7 1. des, de
2. des, de
3. des, de
4. des, de
5. des, Des
6. des, de

Leçon B

8 1. F 2. H 3. K 4. I 5. G 6. A 7. D 8. J 9. L 10. C 11. E 12. B

9 Answers will vary.

10 rez-de-chaussée, sous-sol, salon, cuisine, chambre, premier étage, fleurs, arbres, voiture, garage

11 1. prends, prends
2. prenez, prenons
3. prennent, prends
4. prenez, prenons
5. prennent, prennent
6. prend, prends

12 1. apprend
2. apprennent
3. apprenons
4. apprends
5. apprenez
6. apprennent
7. apprends
8. apprend

13 1. Nous ne comprenons pas l'allemand.
2. Pete ne comprend pas le chinois.
3. Ben et son demi-frère ne comprennent pas le russe.
4. Les filles du professeur de maths ne comprennent pas l'italien.
5. Vous ne comprenez pas le suédois.
6. Je ne comprends pas le japonais.
7. Tu ne comprends pas le portugais.
8. Terry ne comprend pas le français.

14 1. apprends, apprends
2. comprend, comprend
3. prennent, prend
4. apprend, comprennent
5. prennent, prends

15 1. Mange une salade!
2. Prends de l'eau!
3. Ne fais pas de roller dans la maison!
4. Ne téléphone pas en Allemagne!
5. Joue avec le chien!
6. Va dans ta chambre!
7. Finis tes devoirs!
8. Étudie pour l'interro!

16 1. Écoutez les cassettes en français!
2. N'écoutez pas le rock!
3. Ne parlez pas avec vos amis!
4. Ne mangez pas en classe!
5. Prenez vos cahiers!
6. Ne donnez pas vos interros aux autres élèves!
7. Finissez vos devoirs pour demain!
8. Ne faites pas les devoirs de maths!

17 1. Parlons français!
2. Écoutons la techno!
3. Dansons!
4. Regardons une vidéocassette en français!
5. Prenons des apéros!
6. Mangeons de la pizza!
7. Jouons au foot demain!
8. Allons au concert ensemble!

Leçon C

18
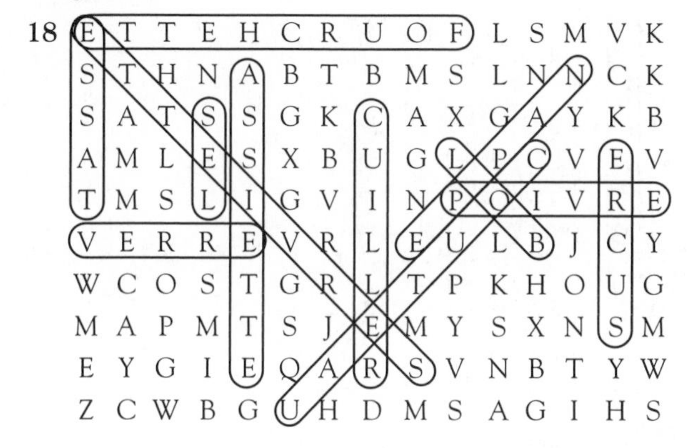

19 Drawings will vary.

20 Answers will vary.

21 Answers will vary.

22 1. mettent
2. mettons
3. mettez
4. mettent
5. mets
6. met
7. mets

23 1. Papa et moi, nous mettons le tapis dans le salon.
2. Amine et toi, vous mettez le canapé dans le séjour.
3. Karim et son frère mettent le grand lit dans notre chambre.
4. Tu mets ton bureau dans ta chambre.
5. Nora et sa sœur mettent les assiettes dans le placard.
6. Latifa met la stéréo dans le séjour.
7. Je mets mes robes dans l'armoire.

24 1. mettez des bottes, un anorak et un pantalon
2. mettent un tee-shirt, un short et des tennis
3. mettons un sweat et un jean
4. met une chemise et un costume
5. met une robe
6. mets un maillot de bain
7. mets une chemise et un pantalon

25 1. mets
2. promets
3. permet
4. promettons
5. mettent
6. promettons
7. permettent
8. promettent

Unité 10

Leçon A

1

2
1. la tête
2. le cou
3. l'épaule
4. le bras
5. le genou
6. la jambe
7. le doigt de pied
8. le pied
9. le doigt
10. la main
11. le dos

3
1. avons chaud
2. ont froid
3. a chaud
4. as froid
5. ai peur
6. ai froid
7. a peur
8. avez chaud

4 1. E 2. H 3. D 4. A 5. F 6. B 7. C 8. G

5
1. Il faut manger beaucoup de fruits.
2. Il ne faut pas prendre de l'alcool.
3. Il ne faut pas manger beaucoup de chips.
4. Il faut prendre de l'eau avec les repas.
5. Il ne faut pas regarder la télé dix heures par jour.
6. Il faut mettre des vêtements confortables.
7. Il faut porter de bons tennis.
8. Il faut dormir huit heures par jour.

6
1. Il faut prendre assez d'euros pour le weekend.
2. Il ne faut pas arriver après 20h00 vendredi soir.
3. Il faut aller au supermarché samedi matin.
4. Il faut préparer un bon déjeuner samedi.
5. Il faut mettre la table.
6. Il faut regarder le match de foot à la télé avec votre grand-père.
7. Il ne faut pas écouter le rock.
8. Il ne faut pas retourner après 22h00 dimanche soir.

7 Answers will vary.

Leçon B

8

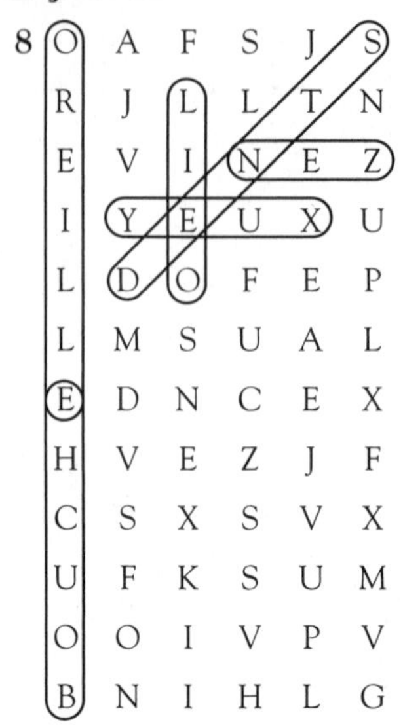

9
1. la bouche
2. les dents
3. le nez
4. l'oreille
5. les yeux
6. l'œil

10
1. quelqu'un, personne
2. toujours, plus
3. quelque chose, rien
4. souvent, jamais

11 Possible answers:
1. veux, peux
2. vas, vais
3. aimes
4. vas, viennent
5. faut
6. préférez, préfère

12 Answers will vary.

13 Answers will vary.

14 1. Mon frère a toujours mal aux dents.
2. J'attends quelqu'un après les cours.
3. Tu ne fais plus de roller.
4. Nous voulons acheter quelque chose pour son anniversaire.
5. Maxine ne trouve rien au centre commercial.
6. Ces élèves ne font jamais leurs devoirs vendredi soir.
7. Il n'y a personne au cinéma ce soir.
8. Ses tantes arrivent toujours après le dessert.
9. Henri étudie souvent à la maison.

15 1. E 2. D 3. B 4. F 5. A 6. C

16 1. Mes amis ne jouent plus au foot.
2. Nous ne faisons rien.
3. Jean-Pierre et moi, nous ne prenons jamais le petit déjeuner le matin.
4. Le professeur ne parle à personne après les cours.
5. Tu ne regardes plus la télé le samedi matin.
6. Maman n'achète rien au marché.
7. On ne skie jamais en juillet.
8. Il n'y a personne dans la cuisine.

17 Answers will vary.

Leçon C

18

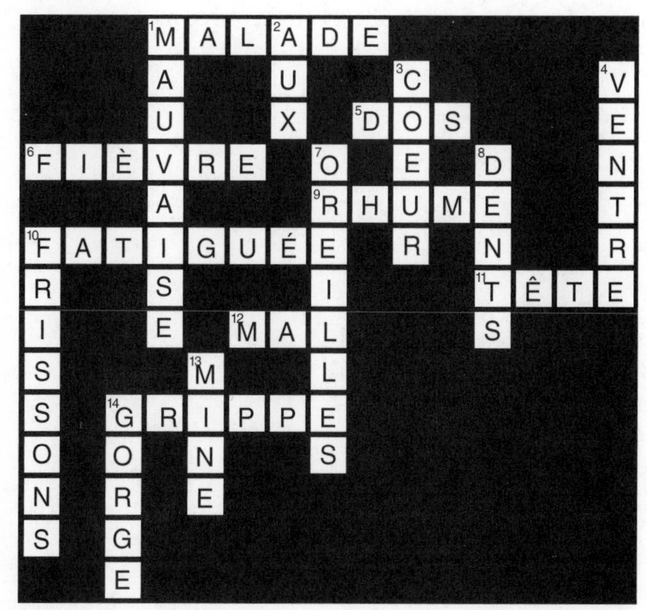

19 En bonne santé: Mlle Fournier n'est pas en mauvaise forme. Charles a bonne mine. Zakia n'a pas mal au cœur. Hervé n'a pas de frissons. Nadine n'a pas mal au ventre.

En mauvaise santé: Théo a la grippe. Karima est en mauvaise forme. Mahmoud est fatigué. Myriam a un rhume. Thierry a mal à la gorge.

20 1. forme, fatigué
2. grippe, ventre, fièvre
3. mine, malade
4. frissons, rhume
5. dos, épaules
6. gorge

21 1. A 2. E 3. G 4. H 5. C 6. D 7. F 8. B

22 1. C 2. H 3. E 4. A 5. D 6. B 7. G 8. F

23 1. devons
2. dois
3. devons
4. dois
5. devons
6. dois
7. devez
8. dois

24 1. Ousmane et Salim doivent acheter de nouveaux cahiers.
2. Tu dois acheter une nouvelle disquette.
3. Monique doit acheter de nouveaux crayons.
4. Zohra et toi, vous devez acheter de nouvelles cassettes.
5. Paul doit acheter un nouveau calendrier.
6. La prof doit acheter un nouvel ordinateur.
7. Nous devons acheter de nouveaux sacs à dos.
8. Moi, je dois acheter une nouvelle trousse.

25 Answers will vary.

Unité 11

Leçon A

1

2
1. Il est belge.
2. Elle est luxembourgeoise.
3. Elles sont suisses.
4. Ils sont belges.
5. Elles sont françaises.
6. Ils sont luxembourgeois.
7. Il est suisse.
8. Ils sont français.

3
1. Mexique
2. Japon
3. Italie
4. Chine
5. Allemagne
6. Luxembourg
7. États-Unis
8. Espagne
9. Belgique
10. Suisse

4
1. sont venues
2. êtes venues
3. est venue
4. sont venus
5. est venu
6. es venue
7. sont venus
8. es venu

5
1. sont sorties
2. sommes rentrés
3. suis resté(e)
4. sont venus
5. est partie
6. êtes allés
7. est arrivée
8. es entrée

6 est venue, est arrivée, est entrée, est rentré, sommes allés, sont sortis, sommes restées, est partie

7
1. Charles, tu n'es pas parti pour prendre le bus à 7h00 le matin.
2. Latifa et Anne, vous n'êtes pas sorties de la maison à 7h30.
3. Nous ne sommes pas arrivés en cours à 8h00.
4. Anne et Claire ne sont pas venues à la cantine.
5. Stéphanie n'est pas entrée dans le fast-food à midi.
6. Je ne suis pas allé(e) étudier avec mes amis.
7. Alexandre n'est pas rentré à 20h00.
8. David et Louis ne sont pas restés à la maison jeudi soir.

8 1. Laïla et Karine êtes-vous restées à la maison pour regarder la télé?
2. Jean-François es-tu rentré de vacances?
3. Assane es-tu allé au cinéma?
4. Jean et Pierre êtes-vous partis avec Thierry?
5. Michèle et Françoise êtes-vous arrivées à la maison à minuit?
6. Arabéa es-tu sortie avec tes parents?
7. Sophie es-tu venue à la boum?
8. Robert et Malika êtes-vous entrés dans le fast-food?

9 Answers will vary.

Leçon B

10

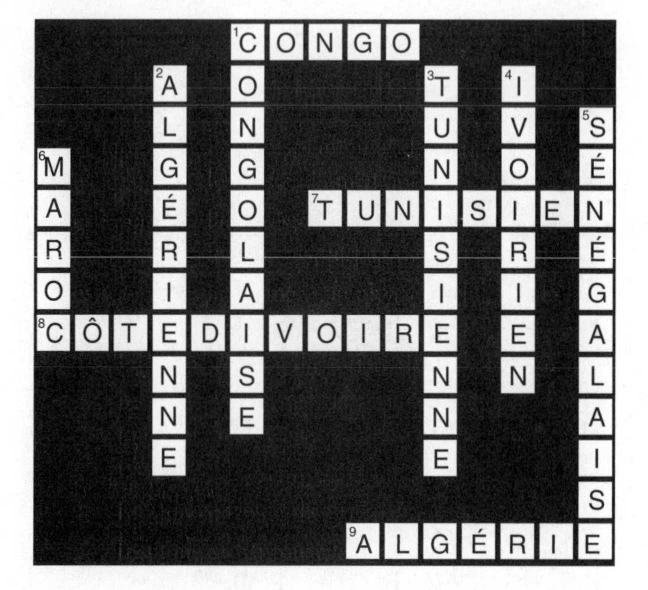

11 1. Luxembourg
2. Côte-d'Ivoire
3. Sénégal
4. Tunisie
5. Maroc
6. Afrique
7. Belgique

12 1. neuvième
2. quatrième
3. dixième
4. premier
5. septième
6. troisième
7. huitième
8. cinquième

13 1. Paola Caprioli est la quatrième.
2. Thérèse Milo est la cinquième.
3. Karine Renaudet est la deuxième.
4. Isabelle Paganelli est la septième.
5. Andrée Riva est la neuvième.
6. Sonia Poitras est la troisième.
7. Gabrielle Blondel est la première.
8. Delphine Lannion est la huitième.

14 Le Suisse est le deuxième.
Le Luxembourgeois est le troisième.
Le Mexicain est le quatrième.
Le Français est le cinquième.
L'Américain est le sixième.
Le Canadien est le septième.
Le Japonais est le huitième.
L'Anglais est le neuvième.

15 1. Il habite à Madrid.
2. Elle habite à Dakar.
3. Elle habite à Paris.
4. Il habite à Bruxelles.
5. Elle habite à Rome.
6. Il habite à Genève.
7. Elle habite à Orlando.
8. Il habite à Abidjan.

16
1. En Tunisie il y a beaucoup de Tunisiens.
2. Au Sénégal il y a beaucoup de Sénégalais.
3. Au Maroc il y a beaucoup de Marocains.
4. En Belgique il y a beaucoup de Belges.
5. Aux États-Unis il y a beaucoup d'Américains.
6. En Algérie il y a beaucoup d'Algériens.
7. Au Canada il y a beaucoup de Canadiens.
8. En Côte-d'Ivoire il y a beaucoup d'Ivoiriens.

17 à, en, au, à, en, à, à, en, aux, à

Leçon C

18

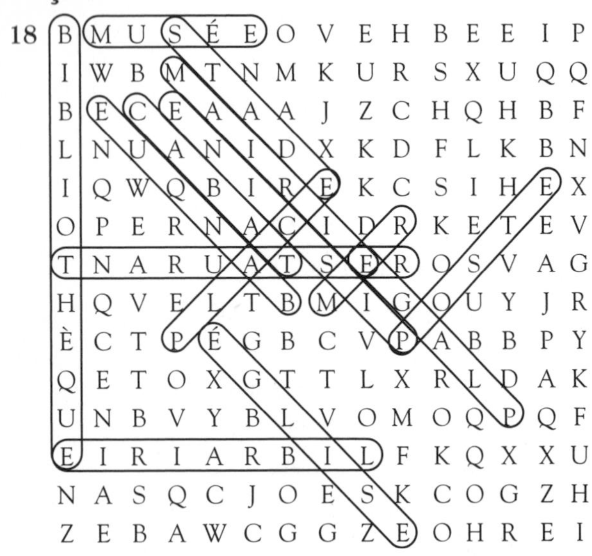

19

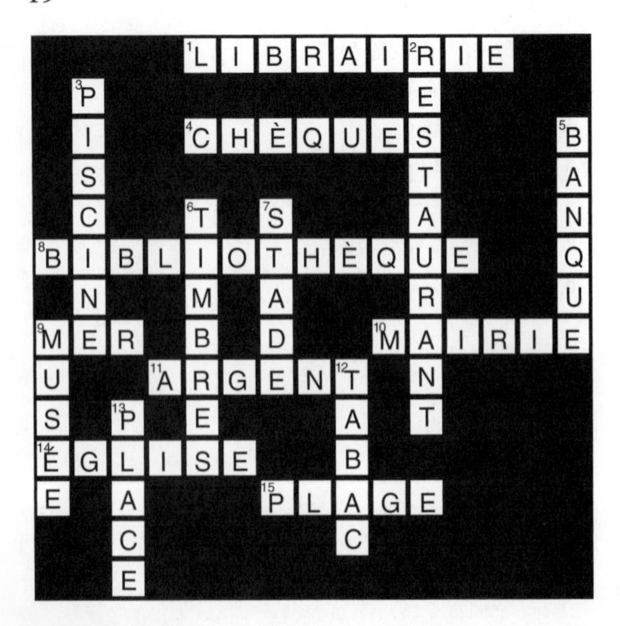

20 1. D 2. H 3. G 4. A 5. E 6. B 7. F 8. C

21 Answers will vary.

22 Answers will vary.

23 Answers will vary.

24
1. voient
2. vois
3. voient
4. voyons
5. vois
6. voyez
7. voit
8. voit

25 Answers will vary.

Unité 12

Leçon A

1

2

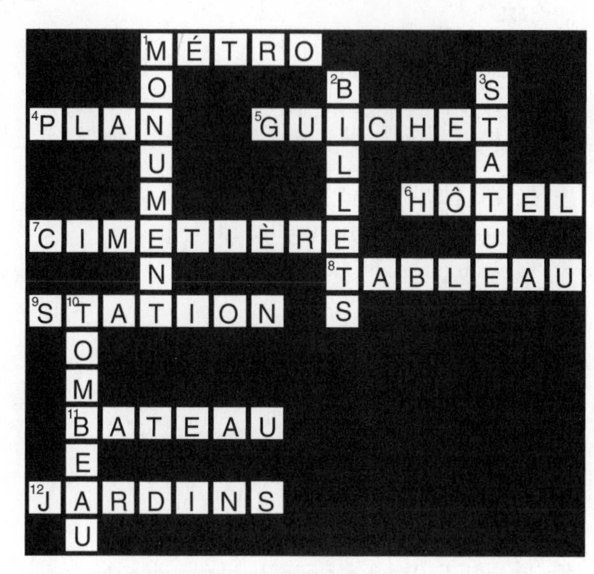

3
1. avez étudié, avons étudié
2. ai étudié, as étudié
3. a étudié, ont étudié
4. ont étudié, a étudié

4
1. n'ont pas étudié, ont voyagé
2. n'avons pas étudié, sommes rentré(e)s
3. n'ont pas étudié, ont préféré
4. n'as pas étudié, as travaillé
5. n'avez pas étudié, êtes resté(e)s
6. n'ai pas étudié, ai invité
7. n'a pas étudié, a gardé
8. n'ont pas étudié, sont allés

5 1. ont choisi 2. avez choisi 3. a choisi 4. avons choisi 5. ont choisi 6. ai choisi 7. a choisi 8. as choisi

6
1. avons attendu
2. ont attendu
3. ont attendu
4. avez attendu
5. a attendu
6. a attendu
7. as attendu
8. ai attendu

7
1. ai attendu, est, venue
2. avons regardé, a dormi
3. a passé, sommes allés
4. sont allés, ont, dansé
5. avez commencé, avez, fini
6. a acheté, a décidé
7. es parti(e), êtes entrés
8. a joué, a perdu

8 Answers will vary.

9 Answers will vary.

Leçon B

10
1. une rue
2. un défilé
3. une musicienne
4. un bal
5. un feu d'artifice
6. un musicien

11 passer, bal, rue, musiciens, jusqu'à, défilé, Champs-Élysées, feu d'artifice, fête, chargés

12 1. a eu 2. ont eu 3. avez eu 4. avons eu 5. ai eu 6. ont eu 7. a eu 8. as eu

13
1. a fait un dessert
2. ont fait du camping
3. ai fait du baby-sitting
4. a fait du vélo
5. avez fait du roller
6. avons fait le tour
7. ont fait les devoirs
8. as fait du shopping

14
1. avons pris, avez pris
2. a pris, ai pris
3. as pris, ai pris
4. ont pris, ont pris
5. avez pris, ai pris
6. a pris, as pris

15 1. as vu, avons vu
2. avez vu, ont vu
3. as vu, a vu
4. ai vu, as vu
5. avez vu, avons vu
6. ont vu, ont vu

16 1. ont fait 2. avez vu 3. as pris 4. sont rentrés 5. ont été 6. sommes allé(e)s 7. ai eu 8. a acheté

17 Answers will vary.

Leçon C

18

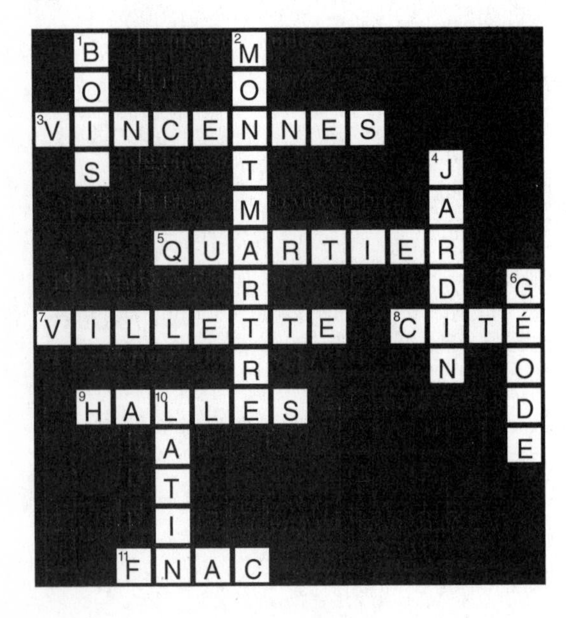

19 1. I 2. H 3. D 4. A 5. G 6. J 7. E 8. F 9. C 10. B

20 1. Elle est allée au Louvre.
2. Ils sont allés à la Sainte-Chapelle.
3. Tu es allé à la Défense.
4. Elles sont allées à la Seine.
5. Il est allé à Montmartre.
6. Vous êtes allé(e)s aux Champs-Élysées.
7. Je suis allé(e) à la tour Eiffel.
8. Nous sommes allés au musée d'Orsay.

21 1. C'est la plus belle affiche.
2. C'est la plus jolie voiture.
3. C'est la jupe la plus courte.
4. C'est le plus petit musée.
5. C'est l'ordinateur le plus cher.
6. C'est la femme la plus généreuse.
7. C'est l'élève le plus intelligent.
8. C'est le plus vieil homme.

22 1. Mon père a le plus grand bateau du monde!
2. Ma grand-mère est la femme la plus généreuse du monde!
3. J'ai le plus joli vélo du monde!
4. Nous avons acheté la voiture la plus formidable du monde!
5. Et moi, j'ai le grand-père le plus sympa du monde!
6. Mon oncle a acheté le tableau le plus cher du monde!
7. Ma sœur et moi, nous avons les jeux vidéo les plus intéressants du monde!
8. Ma mère est la dentiste la plus diligente du monde!

23 Answers will vary.

24 Answers will vary.

25 Answers will vary.